The Culture Crafters

An In-Depth Look at How Pop Culture Seduces Today's Youth and How to Counter Its Influence

by

Randy L. Ballard

authorHOUSE™

1663 LIBERTY DRIVE, SUITE 200
BLOOMINGTON, INDIANA 47403
(800) 839-8640
WWW.AUTHORHOUSE.COM

First published by AuthorHouse 12/15/04

ISBN: 1-4184-9592-1 (sc)
ISBN: 1-4184-9593-X (dj)

Library of Congress Control Number: 2004096929

Printed in the United States of America
Bloomington, Indiana

This book is printed on acid-free paper.

Unless otherwise indicated, the majority of scriptual texts are taken from the King James Version.
Scripture quotations marked GNB are taken from the Good News Bible translation.
Scripture quotations marked MKJV are taken from the Modern King James Version.
Scripture quotations marked NIV are taken from New International Version.
Scripture quotations marked MSG are taken from The Message translation.
Scripture quotations marked ASV are taken from the American Standard Version.
Scripture quotations marked ISV are taken from the International Standard Version.

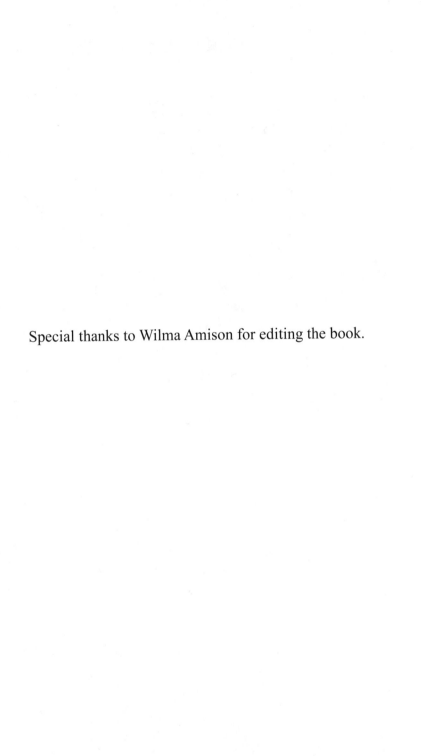

Special thanks to Wilma Amison for editing the book.

I am indebted to my wife, Annette, who
has stood by my side for almost 25 years of marriage and ministry.
She is truly my main source of human inspiration, encouragement, and strength. I am
grateful to her and my son, Gabriel, for allowing me to give myself to this venture.
I love you both and I am thankful to God for every day, hour, and minute we spend
together. May our lives bring glory and honor to Almighty God!

This book is dedicated to my mom and dad, Don and Delores Ballard.
As I was growing up, they believed in me. They often told my brother, sister, and me, that
if we would put God first in our lives, He would use us greatly. Many times throughout my life,
those words have served as a fixed point of reference. I love them both, and I follow Christ
today because of the incarnate Christ that I witnessed in their lives.

Table of Contents

CRAFTING THE CULTURE

Chapter One

The soldiers in the greatest and most powerful army in America do not wear uniforms or carry weapons. In some ways, however, this army does resemble that of Uncle Sam. It is made up of millions of Americans—intellectuals and uneducated, black and white, Democrats and Republicans, rich and poor, religious and non-religious. They have been in training now for over a generation—a training that begins in infancy and continues throughout a lifetime.

From the outside, this army's diversity is striking. But it's in the cultural mind-set of the individuals who comprise this army—their ideas, beliefs, values and actions—that they share an astonishing commonality. These soldiers would be quick to boast of their independence and their differences. Nonetheless, it's the uniformity within their belief system that makes them such a powerful, invisible force.

Who is this army? The American popular culture. What is at the core of its system of beliefs? The apostle Paul inspired by the Holy Spirit summed it up best nearly two thousand years ago: "They exchanged God's truth for a lie and worshipped and served the creation rather than the Creator, who is blessed forever. Amen" (Romans 1:25).

Defining a Culture Crafter

Within our culture today, many with great skill are attempting to deceive and mislead an entire generation away from the Judeo-Christian ethics on which America was founded. These are "the culture crafters."

Two definitions for the word *craft* are "skill in doing or making something, as in the arts; proficiency" and "skill in evasion or deception; guile." The apostle Paul warns us to beware of those who would try to seduce or lead us away from the Christian faith through their philosophies, ideas, opinions and deceit: "Beware lest any man spoil you through philosophy and vain deceit, after the tradition of men, after the rudiments of the world, and not after Christ" (Colossians 2:8).

Dr. James Dobson, of Focus on the Family, said in a recent letter, "The world into which today's children are born has become a very dangerous place. It has changed tremendously. . . .

"The culture is at war with parents. It is very difficult to get kids safely through adolescence. . . . We're seeing a relentless attack on childhood today. There are many people in the activist community who hate the Judeo-Christian system of values, and recognize that if they can gain control of children, they can change the entire culture in one generation. That's why there is a tsunami of propaganda flooding over our culture."

There have never been so many different inducements within our culture reaching out to lure our children. Until the 1960s, youth were primarily influenced by parents, teachers, and maybe a Sunday school teacher or a pastor. Most imitated what they learned from people in the community whose character was known and considered trustworthy by its citizens. However, today's youth culture is targeted by just about everyone and everything—from makers of fast food to fast cars, from clothing designers to unclothed models, from music to movies, from book authors to drug pushers. Whether they live next-door or a continent away, they all have passage into our children's lives, peddling their hollow and deceptive philosophies.

Connie Neal, in her excellent book *Walking Tall in Babylon,* writes, "No longer is it enough to keep ourselves and our kids away from places where we know there is danger, whether physical or moral. The enemy is attacking with aggressive immorality that comes unbidden, intruding into formerly 'safe' places where our families study, work, play, and live."

That's why parents, pastors, educators and anyone who works with youth need to heed the warning of the apostle Paul to beware of the masquerades of today's culture crafters. Parents must exercise Biblical discernment and teach children how to separate between the voices of truth and deception. The writer of Hebrews tells us that not just any parent has the ability to do this: "Solid food, on the other hand, is for adults, who through practice are able to distinguish between good and evil" (Hebrews 5:14, *GNB*).

It is a daily diet of God's Word that gives us the ability to teach Biblical discernment to our children. The psalmist David understood this when he wrote, "Behold, thou desirest truth in the inward parts: and in the hidden part thou shalt make me to know wisdom" (Psalm 51:6). David was simply saying that God's Word must be internalized if we want His Spirit to make a difference in our lives as well as in the lives of those around us.

Postmodernism's Influence

Recently, the American pop culture seems to be taking its cues from a school of thought known as postmodernism. This new era has been characterized by a rejection of absolute truths and previous popular narratives that have attempted to explain the progressive evolution of society. At the same time it has brought to the surface a multitude of different perspectives on society and an appreciation of different cultures. It highlights globalization and multiculturalism, but it also underscores an appreciation for commonality.

Postmodernists hold to the view that human beings are largely products of their culture, that our identity is defined by our culture (African-American, European, Eastern, suburbia, urban, Jewish, etc.). Dr. Gene Edward Veith, in an article written for *Teachers in Focus* magazine (a publication of Focus on the Family), wrote,

"Postmodernists see truth as a construction. The postmodernists would say, "We build 'plausibility structures'—conglomerations of stories, beliefs, commitments and presuppositions—to help us understand our experiences and give our lives meaning." In other words, our personal "beliefs make up what we have been conditioned to accept by our society, just as others have been conditioned to accept a completely different set of beliefs. Nonetheless, these man-made structures cannot lead them to absolute truth. They are always breaking down and always changing."

Research shows that postmodernism is making a profound impression on how today's youth perceive and process objective truths. How have parents, pastors and educators countered the influence of postmodernism? We have not; it has caught us completely off guard.

How Pop Culture Influences

How does popular culture lure and charm the masses? Benno Muller Hill says, "The majority of the masses look for security and safety. They figure if a lot of people are doing something, it must be right. If most people accept it, then it probably represents fairness, equality, compassion, and sensitivity."

Setting and following trends is a characteristic of all cultures. Today's popular culture influences the cars we drive, our stock market picks, the clothes we buy, the movies and television programs we view, the restaurants we frequent, the medicines we take, the homes we buy, the trips we take, the sports we play, the books we read, the indebtedness that's on our credit cards—and, yes, even our values and standards are now determined by pop culture, better known as political correctness.

Life is much simpler when we just go along with the trends. It requires less thinking and work. We don't have to worry about standing out. If we go along with pop culture, we just blend in with everyone else.

The media takes polls and conducts surveys, and whatever the majority says is treated as truth or what's best for everyone. But history demonstrates that the majority is not always right. Today's pop culture ignores and often reviles objective truth. Therefore, their views are often wrong, even if they are shared by a majority of their peers.

Jesus explained pop culture's appeal by comparing it to a broad road that many people travel down but which eventually leads to eternal destruction (Matthew 7:13). It is the easy way. It is the road of least resistance, and it appeals to the majority. However, Jesus also spoke of another path. A narrow road, with few traveling on it. Jesus said this road leads to life—here on earth, and afterward, eternal life (v. 14).

Jesus warned in the next verse, "Beware of false prophets, which come to you in sheep's clothing, but inwardly they are ravening wolves." Jesus' warning is similar to Paul's: "Beware, lest any man spoil you through philosophy and vain deceit" (Colossians 2:8). Both Jesus and Paul are not only making reference to leaders of religious organizations or cults. But they are also cautioning against the majority in society, those in mainstream culture who gravitate toward popular man-made philosophies and appealing ideas. This broad, convenient and acceptable way is the road of deception that Jesus warned leads to destruction.

How Ideas Are Processed

How do today's culture crafters get their ideas to the masses? How do they persuade the culture to buy into philosophies and beliefs that are not factual?

Gregory Kóukl and Francis Beckwith, in their book *Relativism*, explain the process: "Ideas that are whispered are seldom analyzed well, for they simply don't draw enough attention. By means of repetition and passive acceptance over time, they take on the force of common wisdom, a 'truth' that everyone knows but no one has stopped to examine . . . a kind of intellectual urban legend.

When ideas like these take root, they are difficult to dislodge. The ideas become so much a part of our emerging intellectual constitution that we are increasingly incapable of critical self-reflection. Even if we did, we have little conviction that such analysis would do any good anyway."

It is astounding how the "intellectual urban legends" or the lies of certain culture crafters have shaped the thinking and beliefs of the American culture. Take a look below at the various social movements and their erroneous ideas that have become accepted as common truths by the populace.

Pro-Choice Movement—A woman's right to choose supersedes the right of life for the child in her womb.

Gay Movement—Homosexuality is genetic; most gay men and women are born that way.

Entertainment/Media— Art can only influence society for good, not for ill.

Sexual Revolution/Humanism—Short of harming others or compelling them to do likewise, individuals should be permitted to express their sexual proclivities and pursue their lifestyles as they desire.

Humanism—Happiness, the good life, individuality and shared enjoyments are continual themes of human life. Man at the core of his nature is basically good.

Darwinism/Evolution—Man evolved from advanced forms of animals, mainly from monkeys.

Relativism —All truth is relative, subjective. There are no absolute truths or standards that apply universally.

Shockingly, some, if not most, of the Protestant churches in America recognize these so-called "common truths." George Barna in *What Americans Believe*, points to research that show the church's ethics often mirror pop culture's ethics. With regard to some of these beliefs, the church is even more liberal than the non-Christian population. For example, 73 percent of Protestant Christians when surveyed said they do not believe in absolute truth compared to 65 percent of non-Christians. It looks like the culture crafters are making inroads in what has historically been known as the most conservative segment of American society, the church.

Who Are the Culture Crafters?

George Barna, a religious pollster and author, says it's obvious that the church in America is not penetrating the culture. Ravi

Zacharias agrees: "We (the American church) have isolated ourselves philosophically and socially in the last 10 to 20 years." Barna says the major forces impacting the culture today are movies, television, the Internet, public policy, family, education, books and music. For good or for ill, these comprise the majority of the culture crafters of the 21st century. Barna's research is not surprising considering the following facts:

- The average American child spends four to eight hours a day watching **television.** That's one-fourth to two-fifths of the hours they are not sleeping. CBS sold a 30-second commercial during the 2003 Super Bowl for a record sum of $3 million. The fact is, television sells products and ideas. It's insane to suggest that television is not persuasive!

- Much of Hollywood's multibillion dollar **movie industry** is aimed at high school and college students. Movies are, by their very nature, powerful messengers. They can teach truth, or they can influence us in a negative way. We cannot remain separate and unaffected by the big screen.

- The **Internet** is here to stay, and it continues to make a profound impression upon our culture. One Florida university study recently revealed that one-third of all divorces in America can be traced to online infidelity. The study found that almost one-third of those who start an affair online end up meeting in person.

- **Public policy issues** such as the sanctity of life, homosexuality, divorce, sexual purity, terrorism and child pornography greatly shape and impact the present and future lives of our children.

- In a day when blended families and single-parent families outnumber nuclear families, **the family** is often still the most influential force in a child's life. In the midst of all the voices of culture vying for today's youth, Dad and Mom's opportunities to shape and mold their child remain fixed.

- As we have already understood, sowing ideas always reaps consequences. John Dewey's experimental and pragmatic theories of **education** first introduced in 1933, has led to much of the of the present predicament of public education. Mr. Dewey hammered out the first *Humanist Manifesto* which undergirded his claims that "truth is relative," and is responsible for laying the groundwork for relativism and its infamous *values clarification* experiment of the '60s and '70s.

• Even though it seems many of today's youth culture would choose torture over reading, **books** such as those included in the *Harry Potter* series are profoundly impacting today's children. The *Harry Potter* book series topped 48 million copies sold within the first four years, with editions in 110 countries. There is no question the series has awakened a love of reading among children unparalleled in this generation. But it's the content of the *Harry Potter* books that should alarm parents, especially those with Judeo-Christian values. The Bible clearly warns us in Deuteronomy 18:10-12, not to practice divination, or look for omens, or use spells or charms, and forbids from consulting the spirits of the dead. When we as a culture train and condition our children in such vile and desecrating practices, we are making gigantic deposits in a future that will be characterized by demonic oppression and demonic activity unlike America has ever seen.

• **Music** is a religion in the American pop culture. When most American youth are not in the classroom or in front of the small or large screen, they will likely be found listening to some kind of tune on a radio or CD player. Recent studies show that music can affect the behavior of teens. In 1997, Senator Joe Lieberman stated before a Governmental Affairs Committee, "We don't seem to blink when prominent corporate citizens sell music to our children that celebrates violence, including the murder of police, gang rape, and sexual perversity, including pedophilia. Surreal though it seems, these cultural indicators have very real implications."

Building the Best Defense Possible

To this point, I have painted only a frightening and discouraging portrait of popular culture, but in future chapters not only will I continue to expose today's culture crafters, but I will also offer some sound, practical Scriptural principles that are vital in preventing them from gaining control of our children. In the chapters on countering the culture, I illustrate those principles with stories of both Biblical and modern-day characters who prove to be bigger than the popular culture of their day. These stories of courageous men and women are meant to inspire discernment between the truth and Satan's lies, help point out those lies, and counteract the deception of today's culture crafters.

Do our children have a chance? Absolutely! But without question, parents are the key. For that reason, much of the Biblical prevention principles address moms and dads.

Recently, I heard on an *Injoy* tape (John Maxwell's cassette tape club) that Dr. Charles Stanley daily told his son, Andy, that God had a great plan for him and would one day do something great with his life. Today, Andy Stanley is the founder and pastor of one of America's fastest growing churches in Atlanta, Georgia. I am a proponent of speaking positively and encouragingly to children. Children have a tendency to form a perception of their self-worth from the way those closest to them speak to them and of them.

Christian parents, pastors, teachers, coaches and counselors must unite in their efforts to counter the culture crafters of our day, because they cannot be trusted with our children. Isaiah prophesied that when no one calls for justice or pleads for truth, "they trust in vanity, and speak lies; they conceive mischief, and bring forth iniquity" (Isaiah 59:4). Whether culture's crafters realize it or not, they are effective tools in the hands of Satan. He is the real enemy. The Bible reminds us, "We are not fighting against human beings but against the wicked spiritual forces in the heavenly world, the rulers, authorities, and cosmic powers of the dark age" (Ephesians 6:12, *GNB*).

What is driving Hollywood, the media, most of public policy, postmodernism, the Harry Potter craze, and much of the music world is not so much a man-made, organized conspiracy to control your children, but the spirit of antichrist at work in the world today. We Christians like to complain and blame human beings and human organizations for society's ills, when the Bible clearly tells us that supernatural evil forces must be countered by God's supernatural weapons.

Randy L. Ballard

According to 2 Corinthians 10:4-6, God has given every believer spiritual weapons that are "mighty . . . to the pulling down of [Satanic, supernatural] strong holds [fortresses]." Such weapons demolish every form of deceit or human logic (Greek word is *logismos*), and "every high thing that exalts itself against the knowledge of God." These supernatural weapons of God "bring into captivity every thought [intellect, disposition] to the obedience of Christ."

In the chapters ahead, I encourage you to counter pop culture's crafters by employing God's supernatural weapons. As you do this daily, you will build a hedge around your children that no human or evil power can penetrate.

DISCUSSION QUESTIONS

1. Discuss how that Romans 1:25 is at the core of the popular culture's belief system.

2. Do you agree with James Dobson's statement, "The culture is at war with parents." If so, explain how this is true and give examples.

3. Discuss how parents and adults of influence can shape and mold children's' self-worth?

THE IMAGE CRAFTERS

Chapter Two

In Aldous Huxley's *Brave New World*, he envisioned a time in America when people would be controlled by inflicting pleasure. He foresaw a people who would come to love their oppression and adore the technologies that robbed them of their capacity to think. Huxley said that what afflicted people in *Brave New World* was not that they were laughing instead of thinking, but that they did not know what they were laughing about and why they had stopped thinking.

Are we that distant generation Huxley described in *Brave New World*? And if so, has the media (television, the Internet, video games, movies, etc.) reduced us to a mindless society imprisoned by our sensual appetite for pleasures and amusements? As a people, have we really given the media that much predominance over our lives?

When Reading Was Believing

There was once a time in America when reading was the national pastime. People read the Bible as well as other books. They read pamphlets, newsletters, newspapers, Sunday school tracts and posters. Even government documents such as the Federalist Papers were read widely throughout the Northern and Southern states. Novels, too, were a favorite among Americans in the 19th century.

Of Walter Scott's novels, published in 1814 and 1832, Samuel Goodrich wrote: "The appearance of a new novel from his pen caused a greater sensation in the United States than did some of the battles of Napoleon. . . . Everybody read these works, everybody—the refined and the simple."

One might be tempted to think that in those days before electricity brought us more sophisticated forms of entertainment, along with the promise of more leisure time, there wasn't much else to do but read. People worked hard and long hours in those days, mainly on farms. However, it wasn't uncommon to see a young boy reading a book while plowing a field. Afterward, his parents might have taken him and his siblings to the village lecture hall, where capacity crowds would gather to hear famed authors of their day speak. These authors were the American icons of their era. They were not known by their physical appearance, but for the words that they had written.

When Charles Dickens visited America in 1842, his reception equaled the adulation we now give Hollywood personalities, famous athletes and popular rock bands. "I can give you no conception of my welcome," Dickens wrote to a friend. "There never was a King or Emperor upon earth so cheered and followed by the crowds, and entertained at splendid balls and dinners and waited upon by public bodies of all kinds."

America under the influence of the printing press created a public discourse much different from that of today. It was generally more intelligent, solemn and rational, the fruit of a society based on Protestant tradition, which placed a high priority on reading and education—so much so that the Calvinist Puritans made literacy a prerequisite for membership in the church. In 1650 and the years following, New England towns passed laws requiring the maintenance of "reading and writing" schools. By 1660, there were already 444 of these schools in New England, one school for every 12 miles. In the years to come, literacy and book reading became a common practice, and this shaped the American culture for the next two centuries.

This kind of cultural climate allowed for religious discourse in America to flourish, specifically Christianity. The first great national religious "awakening" took place in the middle of the 18th century, led by fiery preachers such as Jonathan Edwards, William Tennant, Theodore Frelinghuysen and George Whitefield. The second great awakening occurred in the middle of the 19th century and was headed by Francis Asbury, Charles Finney, D.L. Moody, and others. This particular awakening was characterized by massive brush-arbor meetings, called "camp meetings," that drew tens of thousands of people to Kentucky and Tennessee for prolonged times of prayer, fellowship and the preaching of God's Word.

Henry Coswell remarked in 1839, "Religious mania is said to be the prevailing form of insanity in the United States." Successful preachers during this era preached with great passion on such topics as hell, judgment, repentance, God's anger, holiness and the second coming of Jesus. In response to their preaching, hearers would weep, shake, run and cry out loud to God.

Were these early American preachers simply backwoods, uncultivated religious salesmen who were using manipulation to persuade a naïve and gullible people? Absolutely not! Just the opposite was true. These were men of great learning and faith in reason, men who were gifted with oratorical and exegetical gifts. Jonathan Edwards was known for reading his sermons, which Daniel Boorstein described as "tightly knit and closely reasoned expositions of theological doctrine." Charles Finney was a trained lawyer who ended his ministerial career as a professor and president of Oberlin College. D.L. Moody and many others went on to found colleges and universities where young people could study theology as well as the arts and sciences.

Without question, the character of discourse in America prior to the 20th century was much different than it is today. It is clear that our forefathers placed great value on the Bible, reading books and learning. Society as a whole was more analytical and scholarly than it is today. Where did that world go? How did the American culture change so drastically and so quickly in the decades that followed?

Seeing Becomes Believing

The invention of the telegraph by Samuel Finley Breese Morse marked the beginning of great changes in America. The telegraph made it possible to move information with rapidity. Morse created a new kind of information grid that allowed public discourse to become unified for the first time in history. Neil Postman wrote in *Amusing Ourselves to Death*, "It introduced a new kind of public conversation. Its language was that of headlines—sensational, fragmented and impersonal. News took the form of slogans, to be noted with excitement, to be forgotten with dispatch. Its language was also entirely discontinuous. One message had no connection to that which preceded or followed it."

The next great event is what Daniel Boorstein, in his pioneering book *The Image*, called "the graphic revolution." According to Postman, "The new imagery, with photography at its forefront, did not merely function as a supplement to language, but bid to replace it as our dominant means for construing, understanding, and testing reality. First in billboards, posters, and advertisements, and later in such 'news' magazines and papers as *Life*, *Look*, the *New York Daily Mirror* and *Daily News*, the picture forced exposition into the background, and in some instances obliterated it altogether. For countless Americans, seeing, not reading, became the basis for believing."

Morse, Edison, Bell and other inventors inspired a 12-year-old boy named Philo Farnsworth. Late one night, young Philo, while hidden away in his attic loft reading old electrical magazines, began to imagine pictures that could fly through the air by radio waves. Later, on a steamy day in the summer of 1921, Philo crisscrossed an open field atop a horse-drawn plowing machine, thinking about television to relieve the boredom, when for a moment he stopped to survey his day's work. Noticing the neatly cut parallel rows in the dirt before him, he was struck with a flash of inspiration—just as he plowed the field back and forth in parallel rows, so could he scan an image, one line at a time, with a magnetically deflected beam of electrons inside a cathode ray tube. At that moment, television as we know it, and all its extensions and further manifestations, arrived on earth in the mind of this 14-year-old farm boy.

Television didn't make its official American domestic debut until after the Second World War. After surviving two wars and a national depression, Americans seemed eager to do more than just fight on foreign soil and work long hours in factories. It was time "to live a little," to laugh, to be entertained. Enter the wonderful world of television, a visual delight, free entertainment inside the home, largely aimed at emotional gratification. Americans were charmed and captivated. Nearly 60 years later, the enchantment shows no sign of waning.

The Power of Imagery

As one psychiatrist has put it, we all build castles in the air. The problems come when we try to live in them, and that didn't happen in a general sense until there was television.

For two generations of Americans, television has served as our babysitter, teacher, companion and friend. Television is not just shaping our culture but has indeed become our culture. Our public understanding of politics, news, sports, education, science, philosophy, and even religion is crafted by television.

Neil Postman comments, "Television has achieved the status of 'myth,' as Roland Barthes uses the word. By myth, he (Barthes) means an understanding of the world that is not problematic, that we are not fully conscious of, that seems, in a word, natural. A myth is a way of thinking so deeply embedded in our consciousness that it is invisible."

Television, movies and the Internet dominate the 21st-century cultural landscape. It has become our means of seeing, understanding and learning about ourselves. It has changed the way we communicate with one another in our schools, workplaces and churches—and in public as well as private settings. Instead of exchanging ideas, people today entertain and inform one another by what they have seen or learned on television. Instead of communicating with substance and meaning, our culture exchanges imagery, accentuating the absurd and the irrational.

In 1999, more video games than books were sold in America. In Japan, video characters are more popular than rock and movie stars. Author Leonard Sweet in *Carpe Manana* wrote, "Today, people are building their lives on the metaphors of the moving images of movies, videos and TV. The image takes precedence over the reality." Good or bad visual images tend to travel with us, which means we can carry with us images that enhance or images that destroy.

To cite a most recent illustration, Michael Moore's movie *Fahrenheit 911*, was seen by millions of Americans throughout the summer of 2004. According to the media and many that saw it, the film contained half-truths and deceptive video clips of the President of the United States and his administration. Whether you liked the film or not, it was powerful propaganda that tattooed on the minds of viewers damaging images of the President. Regrettably, scores of moviegoers interpreted these images as facts. Unquestionably, Michael Moore along with much of Hollywood understands how to utilize the power of imagery.

Images That Provoke Violence

Whether or not television (as well as movies, videos and the Internet) influences our choices and actions has become a foolish and irrelevant argument today. A vast majority of Americans wish the entertainment industry would voluntarily excise some of the sex and violence from television, movies, and most lyrics. According to a UCLA/U.S. News & World Report survey of 6,300 entertainment industry leaders, 87 percent feel violence in the mass media contributes to violence in society.

Medical experts are beginning to acknowledge a connection between the media and violence. In July of 2000, four national health associations (American Medical Association, American Psychological Association, the American Academy of Pediatrics, and the American Academy of Child and Adolescent Psychiatry) issued a joint statement linking the violence in television, music, video games and movies to increasing violence among children. "Its effects are measurable and long lasting. Moreover, prolonged viewing of media violence can lead to emotional desensitization toward violence in real life. The conclusion of the public health community, based on over 30 years of research, is that viewing entertainment violence can lead to increases in aggressive attitudes, values and behaviors in children."

"Television people have put blinders on, and they absolutely refuse—and movie people too—to admit that they can have any influence for ill in our society," says *Wheel of Fortune* host Pat Sajak. "You know the argument: 'We only reflect what's going on; we don't perpetuate it.' And yet not a week goes by in this town that there's not an award ceremony where they're patting each other on the back, saying, 'You raised AIDS awareness' or 'There'll be no more child abuse, thanks to that fine show you did.' The argument is you can only influence for good; you can't influence for ill. That makes no sense at all."

Another way some Hollywood producers and directors justify their obsession with exploitative gore is by branding it as "just fantasy." Fantasy land is what film director Quentin Tarantino calls the setting for his works, *Kill Bill I* and *Kill Bill II*, widely described as the bloodiest feature films ever released by a major studio. Film critic Michael Medved called *Kill Bill I* "a buffet of murder and mayhem with more than 100 performers slaughtered on screen—not just killed, but also horribly mutilated. One gets his tongue chewed off during an attempted rape of the comatose heroine, another dies as his skull is crushed repeatedly in a slamming door. Countless others watch their limbs being sliced off, with the director highlighting splashy (literally) technology that stimulates spurting arteries that spray blood in a delicate, fine mist."

"This is definitely not taking place on Planet Earth," says Tarantino. Medved says the argument ignores the obvious fact that even though fantasies may not kill or maim, they can still corrupt and degrade. "Treating graphic violence as a joke doesn't make it less disturbing or damaging," he maintains.

After the Columbine High School massacre on April 20, 1999, you would have thought that Hollywood and our culture as a whole would be less tolerant of Torantino's brand of sadistic graphic violence that even he calls "black comedy." Nonetheless, among the cultural elite there seems to be a cynicism that refuses to take any responsibility for coarsening cultural sensibilities and eroding its standards. The truth is "fantasy land" corrupts and degrades, and according to today's news headlines, "harmless entertainment" can be anything but harmless.

Consider the case of Mario Padilla, 17, who was found guilty of killing his mother with the aid of his cousin, Samuel Ramirez, 16. Both boys say they were influenced by the film Scream. In a taped confession to police, the boys said they killed and robbed a young lady to get enough money to buy costumes like those used by the killers in the movie. They also told police they intended to wear them when killing several of their classmates. Padilla also said he partly blamed watching television since the age of seven, as well as movies, drama, comedy, and suspense and horror movies. Its ironic that people say, "Don't let your kids watch TV at that age, because it really does affect them. All I would do was fantasize how to do things."

Another story pulled from today's headlines tells of nine year-old Jennifer, who died by hanging herself with a shoelace. Investigators believe she was reenacting a scene from *The Man in the Iron Mask*. Her parents said she had become captivated by the death of a princess who hangs herself in the movie (a 1998 film rated PG-13). Her mother said she had found the girl acting out the movie's death scene twice before.

"Ever since she was four years old, she would act out what she saw in the movies," said Carmen, her mother. "She would play parts from *Anastasia* or *The Hunchback of Notre Dame*. But she always knew the difference between pretend and reality. Until now."

The probability that children's and teenager's behavior will be at least somewhat influenced by television, the Internet, video games and movies is astronomical, especially considering the sheer volume of entertainment that is consumed by today's youth. Over 1,000 studies show that by age 18, a U.S. youth will have seen 16,000 simulated murders and 200,000 acts of violence. This is possible, because the average youth in America watches 25 hours of television each week and plays computer games an additional seven hours per week. Children spend more time watching television than in any other activity except sleep.

How does such a high volume of violent media intake affect the average youth? According to research, children and teens are impacted in several different ways. Research has shown that "mindless" television or video games affect children physically by impoverishing the development of the prefrontal cortex, that portion of the brain that is responsible for planning, organizing and sequencing behavior for self-control, moral judgment and attention. Children are also affected socially. Studies show children often behave differently after they've been watching violent programs on television. Children who watch violent shows are more likely to strike out at playmates, argue, disobey authority and are less willing to wait for things than children who watch nonviolent programs. Also, research indicates that a steady diet of violent content over time creates a culture that tells kids that violence is the accepted way we solve our problems.

Images That Promote Promiscuity

The media uses sex to sell everything from toothpaste to toilet paper. Good-looking faces and hard bodies are strategically utilized to sell products, movies, sports, sitcoms, magazines, politicians, newspapers, ideas, and even local and national news. Computer users are especially targeted with graphic stories and unwholesome photos of television or movie personalities. The interstate is cluttered with billboards using sex to advertise almost everything. Major corporations say the bottom line is that sex sells. But in reality, traditional institutions like marriage and the family are paying the price. Teens themselves confirm TV's impact: 70 percent said television sex influenced the sexual behavior of kids their age (2003 Kaiser Family Foundation).

According to studies and research, almost eight out of every 10 people say that there is too much sex before marriage portrayed on television. "Prime-time TV is saturated with sex," says Vicky Rideout, vice president of the Kaiser Family Foundation. About seven out of 10 shows have sexual content, averaging six sexual references an hour, according to Kaiser's 2003 report. Sixty-two percent says that sex on TV shows and movies influences kids to have sex when they are too young. (According to a 2002 Kaiser study, in considering decisions about contraceptives, STDs and sexual health choices, teens are almost as likely to get their information from TV.)

As if television isn't enough, "infidelity online" has become the latest trend among both teens and adults. A University of Florida study shows that one-third of all divorces in America can now be traced to online infidelity. The study found that many affairs start in chat rooms specifically set up to match people. Yahoo has a chat room called "Married and Flirting," and Microsoft has one titled "Married but Flirting."

"Most people that are married that are in chat rooms do not believe that what they're doing is a form of cheating, is a form of infidelity, at all," said Beatriz Avila Mileham, the university study conductor. The study found that almost a third of those who start an affair online end up meeting in person. Milehan said Internet philandering is on the way to becoming the most common form of infidelity. Its appeal stems from the fact that it is anonymous.

Undoubtedly, the Internet has become the porn industry's main line of commerce. Twelve percent of the 4.2 million Web sites are pornography related. There are 68 million daily search-engine requests, of which 25 percent are pornographic in nature. Every year there are 72 million visitors to pornographic Web sites worldwide. Of those 25 percent, 116,000 are Gnutella "child pornography" requests.

What is most frightening about pornography is its growth and popularity among children and youth. In the U.S. it is illegal for 17-year-olds and younger to purchase obscene videos and magazines or to see movies with pornographic scenes. Now with the rise of the Internet, the primary pornographic consumer group is young boys between 12 and 17 years old. Of the 15-to-17-year-old boys, an alarming 80 percent have had multiple hard-core exposures. Ninety percent of boys 8 to16 years of age said they have viewed pornography online, most while doing their homework.

Pornography Goes Mainstream. "The culture is pornographic. Kids are growing up with an appetite for sexually charged images for entertainment. The generation we are looking at right now has never known a time of innocence," says journalist and author Eric Schlosser. "People were sent to prison in the early 1960s for selling material much tamer than what HBO now shows on a typical night."

Millions of families are reaping the negative effects of sexual perversion that is captured by camera images. Pornography in America is quickly becoming a national epidemic that threatens to destroy what remains of the moral fabric of our nation. Pornography is a $12 billion to $13 billion-a-year industry which is more than the combined annual revenues of the Coca-Cola and McDonnell Douglas corporations. Worldwide, porn video sales alone top 20 billion a year, which means they generate more revenue than all the football, basketball and baseball franchises combined. U.S. porn revenue exceeds the combined revenues of ABC, CBS and NBC ($6.2 billion).

One of the big reasons for modern pornography's cultural recognition, acceptability and prosperity is due to its sleazy but affluent partnership with the entertainment and media industry. San Fernando Valley, California, dubbed "Silicone Valley" for the many "enhanced" female figures among the estimated 9,000 people working in what has become known as the capital of the world's porn industry. Adult Video News, the porn industry's journal, hosts its own glitzy annual version of the Oscars, with trophies awarded for "best scene" performances in a wide variety of categories unprintable here. In addition, pornographers are widely recognized in the entertainment-media technology field for experimenting with how the 8 mm film, then the video, the Internet and interactive DVDs could broaden their market.

With the availability and consumption of pornography multiplying, aberrant ideas, attitudes and behaviors regarding sex will be on the rise. Consequently, so will sexually transmitted diseases, divorce, teenage pregnancy, abortions, government sex-education spending, sex crimes, and HIV/AIDS victims. During the

2004 Super Bowl show, media giant Viacom spent $200 million in the second year of a TV campaign aimed at spreading the word that people are still becoming infected with HIV and dying of AIDS. The pre-Super Bowl ad showed young people climbing out of a trash bin with a voice-over saying that 20 million young people are expected to contract AIDS, "but it doesn't have to be like that."

Sadly, it does have to be like that for those who choose to disregard God's laws, because His Word says, "Do not deceive yourselves; no one makes a fool of God. You will reap exactly what you plant. If you plant in the field of your natural desires, from it you will gather the harvest of death" (Galatians 6:7,8a,*GNB*). But the good news is we are not without hope; there is a solution God says. "If you plant in the field of the Spirit, from the Spirit you will gather the harvest of eternal life" (Galatians 6:8b, *GNB*). America and Americans have been given a choice by God; we can choose either death or life. Everyone gets to make that choice!

Images That Preach Ideas

"As I understand the word, a curriculum is a specifically constructed information system whose purpose is to influence, teach or cultivate the mind and character of youth," writes Neil Postman. "Television, of course, does exactly that, and does it relentlessly. In so doing, it competes successfully with the school curriculum. By which I mean, it [almost completely] obliterates it."

This was illustrated in an opening paragraph of a USA Today article titled, "When 'Friends' Talk, Teens Listen." "One episode of 'Friends' might have taught teenagers more about risky sex than hours of adult preaching and reached far more children than any school's sex education program, as a survey suggests today. A RAND senior behavior scientist, Rebecca Collins, focused her study on an episode of Friends in which Rachael (Jennifer Aniston) told Ross (David Schwimmer) that she was pregnant, even though they had used a condom. The show mentioned twice that condoms are 97 percent effective. About 1.7 million children ages 12 to 17 saw the episode when it aired October 11, 2001, according to Nielsen Media Research. Collins surveyed 506 frequent viewers of Friends, ages

12 to 17, within a few weeks of the episode and then six months later. Her report shows that many got the 'safe sex' facts. About two thirds of viewers recalled how condom failure had resulted in pregnancy."

Whether its early-morning news shows, mid-morning talk shows, daytime soap operas, "Oprah" in the afternoon, early-evening news shows, prime-time sitcoms, or late-night talk shows, television often uses the spotlight to unashamedly preach its subjective ideas and philosophies. Do they have an agenda? You better believe it! And it doesn't take a brain surgeon to figure out what their agenda is all about—to bring about social change in America and to bring down traditional social norms in doing so.

On the youth front, it seems that nobody influences the minds of teenagers more than MTV. In 2000 before the presidential campaign, MTV ran a documentary it called *Choose or Lose 2000: Sex Laws*. More than anything, the program turned out to be a commercial for anything-goes attitudes toward sexuality. It favored "safe sex," abortion and homosexuality, and provided Bush/Gore comparisons that amounted to much more than subliminal Gore endorsements.

"You may think that what you do is nobody's business," a young woman narrator opens, "but if you do it in this country, Uncle Sam will have his say." The message repeats throughout the program: "what you need to know about the sex laws that could change your life forever," "laws that can affect your sex life," "the fate of your reproductive rights may hang in the balance." A male narrator concludes the show with these words: "In case you still haven't gotten the point, you'd better pay attention, because your sexual freedom is at stake."

Choose or Lose is just a small serving of MTV's constant sustenance of propagandistic programming, music videos, and interviews that preach liberal ideas and attack traditional family and Christian values.

Over the last few years, another obsession of television is the promotion of the gay lifestyle. Hollywood is pulling out all the stops to show that homosexual relationships are normal and that gay and lesbian couples make beautiful, cohesive families that contribute to society as a whole. In the fall of 2003, various TV networks joined efforts in running an in-your-face, unabashed pro-gay campaign during prime-time hours. One of the network's big hitters was *Queer Eye for the Straight Guy*, which featured a team of experts who helped transform style-deficient, culture-deprived heterosexuals into dashing dudes. ABC aired a show titled *It's All Relative*, which featured a happily married gay couple as guardian parents of a young liberated woman who marries a man with bigoted parents. Fox debuted *A Minute With Stan Hooper*, which was about a roving TV commentator who settles in a small town where two of the colorful male residents, Peter and Lou, are happily married.

The media uses these TV shows along with many other venues to preach their pro-gay message whether the culture is ready or not to receive it. Fortunately, many of these shows that try to cram ultraliberal views down the viewers' throats don't make it past the first season simply because most people resent television's strong-arm tactics. However, there are many other media urgings that are subtler and less perceptible that influence social behavior within our culture.

To cite an instance, in 2003 a popular fast-food franchise ran a series of commercials using the popular WWJD? (What Would Jesus Do?) question that appears on many Christian bracelets and T-shirts. It's not the use of the WWJD? abbreviation that is offensive to many followers of Christ, but the content of the commercial itself. In the series of commercials, various characters who find themselves in difficult circumstances (one man's house is burning) ask, "What would Jared do?" Jared is the franchise poster child who is credited with losing lots of weight, supposedly by eating at this particular franchise.

Perhaps most people watching the commercial think it's harmless entertainment or just a clever play on words or an idea. However, many Christians see the commercial's creators sarcastically attacking the notion of a Christian asking the question "What would Jesus do?" when faced with difficult circumstances or certain temptations.

Other ideas, beliefs and values that are often accepted and exalted by the media include evolution, moral relativism, tolerance, pluralism, pro-choice, amorality, socialism, sexual freedom, self-indulgence, and the innate goodness of man. Why is the media purposefully attempting to shape the minds, character and behavior of its viewers, especially children and youth? Why don't they just stick to the business of entertainment . . . and objectivity when it comes to reporting the news?

Will the Image Crafters Prevail?

So it looks as if we are all living in Huxley's *Brave New World*. We seem enslaved by our sensual appetite for pleasures and amusements. Undoubtedly, our generation has been reduced to passivity and egoism. Our love affair with "image-like" technologies has consumed us. Truth for many has drowned in a sea of irrelevance. So what's the answer? How do we keep from cultural collapse or disaster? Huxley, Postman, and others have said that education is the answer—that somehow schools could require and make it the center of education to teach children how to distance themselves from the prevailing forms of information (the media). Do we still believe that teaching our children to resist the pressures of the current culture is a viable option? Or have we surrendered to the image crafters? Can the image crafters be successfully countered? And if so, how?

DISCUSSION QUESTIONS

1. What can parents do to protect their children from entertainment violence? What can the church do?

2. What can parents do to protect children from the culture's obsession with sex? What can the church do?

3. What can parents do to protect children from the culture's misleading and deceptive ideas and philosophies? What can the church do?

COUNTERING THE IMAGE CRAFTERS:
Instilling Courage and Conviction

Chapter Three

Daniel 3 tells of Nebuchadnezzar, a Babylonian king, who once built a golden image 90 feet high and 9 feet wide. He then issued a law that when the music began, everyone in his kingdom must bow down and worship this golden image. Shortly after the decree went into effect, there were certain Chaldeans (Babylonians) who noticed that some of the young Jewish men who worked as government administrators were not bowing to the golden image, and these young men—Shadrach, Meshach and Abednego—were immediately reported to the king (3:12).

King Nebuchadnezzar was furious. He commanded that Shadrach, Meshach and Abednego be brought before him. Nebuchadnezzar then said to them, "Is it true that you refuse to worship my god and to bow down to the gold statue I have set up?" (v. 14b, *GNB*).

Before they could answer, the king reminded them of the consequences of their disobedience—they would be thrown into a blazing furnace. He then added, "Do you think there is any god that can save you?" (v.15b, *GNB*).

These three young men had already proven their loyalty to the king, but they refused to be intimidated into obeying the king's command to worship an idol. They replied, "If it is so that our God whom we serve is able to deliver us from the burning fiery furnace, then He will deliver us out of your hand, O king. But if not, let it be known to you, O king, that we will not serve your gods nor worship the golden image which you have set up" (vv. 17, 18, *MKJV*).

When Nebuchadnezzar heard their response, he became even more furious than when he ordered that they be brought before him. Gone was his conciliatory tone. The only thing hotter than Nebuchadnezzar's anger was the furnace, and he ordered that it be heated seven times hotter than normal. He then commanded the strongest soldiers in his army to take Shadrach, Meshach and Abednego and throw them bound and fully dressed into the fire. The Bible says the fire was so hot it burned to death the guards who threw them in.

That is far from the end of the story, however. What happened next horrified the king. He couldn't believe his eyes when he looked into the furnace. He said to his counselors, "Did we not throw three men bound into the middle of the fire?" (v. 24, *MKJV*). The counselors agreed there were three.

"Behold!" said Nebuchadnezzar, "I see four men loose, walking in the middle of the fire, and there is no harm among them. And the form of the fourth is like a son of the gods" (v. 25, *MKJV*).

Certainly, Nebuchadnezzar had never seen the Son of God before. But to him, the fourth person in the fire looked like a son of a supernatural god or angel. He then moved closer to the fiery furnace and called out to the three young men, "Servants of the Most High God, come forth and come here" (v. 26, *MKJV*). The Bible says the three Hebrew men came out from the middle of the fire unburned, with not even the scent of fire on them.

What was Nebuchadnezzar's response? He had seen all he needed to see. He immediately sent out a new law throughout his kingdom: "If anyone of any nation, race, or language speaks disrespectfully of the God of Shadrach, Meshach, and Abednego, he is to be torn limb from limb, and his house is to be made a pile of ruins. There is no other god who can rescue like this" (v. 29, *GNB*).

To Bow or Not to Bow

Like Babylon's Nebuchadnezzar, every culture has its image crafters. The devil operates through magnification and imagery. He deceives by magnifying ideas or personalities to appear greater than what they really are. He has practiced this kind of deception from the very beginning, when he said, "I will exalt my throne above the stars of God . . . above the heights of the clouds. I will be like the most High" (Isaiah 14:13, 14). Jesus called Satan the father of all lies (John 8:44).

Kimberly Daniels, in *Clean House—Strong House*, says, "Imagery is the production of mental images or sounds through erroneous perception arising from misrepresentation, closely related to hallucination, which is mental wondering. . . . Imagery is only real if we receive it to be so. Jesus really has all power, and Satan has to operate with a counterfeit authority. The devil has been stripped of all power."

Human beings have since the beginning created godlike images and desired that others bow down to them. Thankfully, in America we have never been forced by law to pay homage or give worship to others' images. On the other hand, Satan needs no such laws when popular culture voluntarily bows before its adored icons.

Admittedly, the majority in the Western church have neither discerned nor defied modern-day image crafters. Instead, the church has blended in quite well, picking its battles carefully, usually dependent on whether or not a specific battle serves its best interests. In fact, for many who attend church today their rationale and response to the dilemma faced by the three Hebrew young men would probably be similar to the following:

• It depends on what a person is going through at the particular time he hears the music. If things are going well, he doesn't bow. If the devil's giving him a hard time and he decides to bow, there's no need to worry, because God will forgive him and take him back anyway.

• Whether or not people bow when the music is played depends on whom they are with at that time. If it's another Christian, then they should bow only if the other person bows. If they're in the company of an unbeliever, then it's OK not to bow. *You know, I don't want to make a scene or embarrass them, or make them think that I am a spiritual fanatic.*

• Or it might be a combination of both of the above, depending on the situation or how the person is feeling. *Sometimes, I bow; sometimes I don't. It just depends!*

• Yet, there's a larger segment of the modern church today that doesn't even think twice about whether or not to bow. They march to the drumbeat of the culture. They have conformed so much to the ways and views of the world that they have grown indifferent to the things of God. Sadly, they no longer "preserve sound judgment and discernment," as we are warned to do in Proverbs 3:21.

Unquestionably, the greatest challenge that faces the Western church today is teaching and training our children how to engage popular culture without bowing to its images. Daniel, Shadrach, Meshach and Abednego met the challenge in spite of living in a pagan country. Is it possible for our children to do the same? Absolutely, but there are some basic Christian values practiced by these four Hebrew youth that must be modeled, taught and accentuated by parents today. Below are listed five of these that I consider vital if Christian parents are going to produce children who will be courageous and stand up for godly principles even in a pagan and ungodly culture.

They Internalized God's Word

It begins with hearing. Bible historians date Shadrach, Meshach and Abednego's appearance before King Nebuchadnezzar at approximately 604 B.C. The Book of Daniel refers to them as young men, which probably means they were between 16 and 20 years old. The year Hilkiah the priest found "a book of the law of the Lord given by Moses" (2 Chronicles 34:14) was 618 B.C. It's significant to note that the three Hebrew children, along with Daniel, were just beginning to take their first steps when the Word of God was reintroduced to Judah after it had been missing for an entire generation.

The young king Josiah gathered together all the people of Jerusalem and Judah, including the priests and the Levites. He then read all the words from the Book of the Covenant, which had been found in the Temple (2 Chronicles 34:30). Author Connie Neal describes the scene for us:

"Imagine yourself there among that anxious assembly, abuzz with gossip, conjecture, and solemn concerns as they awaited King Josiah. . . . Imagine a young couple, taking turns holding their infant son, Daniel. His mother had to keep him close, since he was still nursing. Among the assembly were the prophet Jeremiah and Huldah the prophetess, sitting with others who loved the Lord. All the families of the royal line were there, among them Daniel's parents and the parents of infants Hananiah, Azariah, and Mishael (Shadrach, Meshach, and Abednego's Hebrew names). King Josiah's sons were there with their mother, Hamutal."

The first time Josiah had heard the commands, blessings and warnings read from Deuteronomy, he repented and humbled himself, tearing his clothes and weeping. Josiah realized that he was hearing the Word of God that was spoken from Moses to the children of Israel before crossing over into the Promised Land. For possibly the first time, he saw how far Israel had drifted from God's holy standards.

As he read from the Book of the Law to his people with a prophetic utterance, he read with great passion, conviction and hope. He believed that as he read, he was planting God's holy seed in young minds and hearts that would turn the nation of Israel back to the one true and living God, Jehovah.

Raising up kids to be conquerors. Like the parents of Shadrach, Meshach, Abednego and Daniel, we too as parents must understand the importance of our families' hearing the Word of God. We are living in a pluralistic nation. Even though there has been a growing emphasis on family over the last 25 years, church attendance in America has fallen drastically. Even more serious is the actual number of people who profess to be Christians but are not actively involved in the spiritual life of a church. As a pastor, I see more and more people isolating themselves from the body of Christ. Many profess to be worshipers of Christ, the Head, but are reluctant to be accountable to His body (the church).

In Hebrews 10:25, strong emphasis is put on not neglecting to assemble together as believers, and to come together even more frequently as we see the Day of the Lord approaching. According to the signs given to us by Jesus in the Gospels, we could easily be the generation that will see the second coming of Christ. God is warning us that as the spirit of antichrist grows more influential on the earth, we need to come together with other believers to hear His Word. Hearing, which implies receiving and obeying, God's Word produces faith (Romans 10:17). Possibly, the parents of the Hebrew boys knew what the apostle John must have known when he penned, "This is the victory that conquers the world, even our faith" (1 John 5:4, *Amplified Bible*).

It continues with teaching and modeling. The internalization of God's Word began with Josiah's reading, but it did not end there. Much earlier, God had charged parents to teach and to pass on His Word to their children: "Remember these commands and cherish them. Tie them on your arms and wear them on your foreheads as a reminder. Teach them to your children. Talk about them when you are at home and when you are away, when you are resting and when you are working. Write them on the doorposts of your houses and on your gates. Then you and your children will live a long time in the land that the Lord your God promised to give to your ancestors. You will live there as long as there is a sky above the earth. Obey faithfully everything that I have commanded you: Love the Lord your God, do everything he commands, and be faithful to him" (Deuteronomy 11:18-22, *GNB*).

It's evident that the parents of the three Hebrew boys, along with Daniel's parents, took God's words to heart. The reading of Deuteronomy from the lips of King Josiah would be just the beginning. We can construe that from that day forward many of the parents present made it their number one priority to train their children in the ways of Jehovah God just as Moses had instructed them to. It was these parents' daily sowing of God's commands into their children that would reap a harvest years later as they dwelled in the midst of a godless, pagan nation.

Very few Christian parents today take the time to disciple, train and equip their children in the Word of God. Some parents seem to think that taking them to a church with a good children's or youth ministry will be enough to assure that when the children are old, they " will not depart from it" (Proverbs 22:6). It takes more than a Sunday-morning church service to produce children that are righteous before God.

The first part of Proverbs 22:6, reads, "Train up a child in the way that he should go." The idea is to initiate, educate and discipline your children in the path or journey God has laid out for each of them as revealed in God's Word. Unquestionably, God has given parents the responsibility to train and model "the way" before their children. The church can teach and preach the gospel and provide fellowship and ministry opportunities to the whole family. But no church, no school, and no ministry can take the place of a parent or parents modeling a vibrant relationship with Jesus Christ. It is the parents' mission to personally pass on to their children the Word of God and model the righteousness of Christ before them.

They Engaged Their Culture

Having been taken into Babylonian captivity, it would have been easy for Daniel and his three Hebrew friends to shy away from being plunged into a strange, pagan culture. Remember, as captives, they were possibly led away in chains, not knowing whether they would ever see their parents again. They could have chosen to resist and not to cooperate with their enemies. Instead, they engaged their new culture, respecting its different beliefs and practices without compromising their own faith in Jehovah God.

The Book of Daniel shows us four young men who trusted in the promises and the protection of their God. Daniel, Shadrach, Meshach and Abednego excelled in knowledge and skill in literature and philosophy. The Bible says, "No matter what question the king asked or what problem he raised, these four young men knew ten times more than any fortuneteller or magician in his whole kingdom" (Daniel 1:20, *GNB*).

When crises did arise, such as King Nebuchadnezzar's troubling dream (ch. 2) and the fiery furnace (ch. 3), God divinely appointed Daniel and his three friends to be exactly where they were. In those trying moments, they turned to the God they had never stopped trusting and serving.

"They did not have to repent of any ungodly interaction with the culture; rather, we see them in a unique position to stand before God on behalf of this king and those living under the threat of death," writes Connie Neal. "We see them ready to enter into God's presence to request compassion for their ungodly peers and troubled pagan king, along with concern that their lives also be spared."

In the end, as Daniel, Shadrach, Meshach and Abednego engaged the Babylonian culture God blessed them, gave them favor with their enemies, and elevated them to positions of responsibility in the kingdom. Although they were young captives from another land, God made them shining stars that reflected His glory for the world to see.

The Bridger generation. Previous generations have been labeled Builders, Boomers and Busters, and now they tell us that those people born from 1988 on will be called "the Bridger" generation. "The Bridger" generation is a fitting name for today's Christian youth, whom God is calling to build a bridge from His kingdom over into a lost and desperate world so that the multitudes may come to Christ. If this is to happen, Christianity in America must cease its subculture ways. For too long, Christian parents and the church have taught youth isolating and defensive concepts to keep them from becoming worldly, placing great emphasis on corporate worship and de-emphasizing discipleship and evangelism. Clearly, we have failed miserably in equipping today's Christian youth to possess an offensive mind-set so that they might encounter their culture with discernment and purpose.

During my preteen and early teen years, my father served as the PFC (Pioneers for Christ) director for the Church of God in Indiana. Once a month various teens throughout the Churches of

God would meet in a designated Indiana town or city on a Saturday. The morning would be given to prayer and instruction, then in the afternoon we would go two-by-two, door-to-door throughout a neighborhood, sharing the gospel with those who would listen. At some point during our presentation, we would invite them to a service that evening at a nearby church or park where the entire PFC team would be ministering.

Frankly, I dreaded those PFC "Saturday Invasions" more than anything in my life. I don't think I ever became comfortable with knocking on the door of a complete stranger and asking, "If you should die today and stand before God, how would you answer Him if He asked, 'Why should I let you into heaven?'" After a long day of doors slammed in our face, dogs chasing us, and people taking the literature just to get rid of us, I realized those Saturday Invasions taught me how to go into the Enemy's territory ready to do battle.

The intense prayer meetings on Saturday mornings, the gospel outlines we memorized, the variety of good and ill experiences we received as we shared the gospel . . . all of these gave us on-the-job training for learning how to be *on the offensive.* Such experiences and lessons became increasingly valuable to me later, as God called me to plant several churches and then to train others to plant churches and to do personal evangelism.

Jesus himself engaged His own culture as a lifestyle. Not only did He model it, but He also taught us to do the same. In the Sermon on the Mount (Matthew, chapters 5-7), He taught us to be salt so that the world would have the opportunity to taste godliness. He taught us to be a light to the world so that men might see our good works and glorify God. In the parable of the Good Samaritan, our Lord instructed us to go out of our way and care for those that have fallen in the ditches of life. In the parables of the lost coin, the lost sheep, and the prodigal son, we are taught not to turn our back on the wayward and those outside the fold or the family of God. In the parable of the great feast, we are taught as Christ's servants to go out into the world and bring in the poor, the crippled, the blind—anyone and everyone.

Jesus clearly commissions every believer, "Go, then, to all peoples everywhere and make them my disciples" (Matthew 28:19, 20, *GNB*). We cannot fulfill the Great Commission without encountering and engaging the culture.

They Consecrated Themselves to God

The chief official of King Nebuchnezzar selected from the Hebrew exiles some of the sharpest young men from the royal and noble families of Judah. These young men were chosen because of their attractiveness, intelligence, teachability, and soundness of mind and body. For three years this group of young men under the direction of Ashpenaz, the King's chief official, served in the royal court and received training in the Babylonian language (Daniel 1).

From this group, Daniel, Shadrach, Meshach and Abednego emerged as the four with a "holy boldness" about them. Daniel was the leader who was determined not to defile himself by eating the king's food or drinking his wine (v. 8), so he asked Ashpenaz if he could be exempt from the king's diet. Daniel said, "Try us out for ten days on a simple diet of vegetables and water. Then compare us with the young men who eat from the royal menu. Make your decision on the basis of what you see" (Daniel 1:12, 13, *MSG*).

Ten days later, they all looked healthier and stronger than the young men who had been eating the royal food and drinking the wine (v.15). From that time forward, the guard let them eat vegetables instead of the food from the royal court. The Bible says God gave these four young men knowledge and skill in literature and philosophy (vv. 17-20). He also gave Daniel the ability to interpret visions and dreams. At the conclusion of the three-year period, Daniel, Shadrach, Meshach and Abednego stood out among the others and knew 10 times more than any of the king's best fortune-tellers or magicians.

These four found favor with both men and God. What made Daniel and his friends stand out from all the rest? It wasn't talent, hard work or intelligence alone. It's the same characteristic that still brings the favor of men and God on young people today. It's called consecration, and this quality causes individuals to stand head and shoulders above the crowd.

The word *consecrate* means "to anoint, sanctify, or devote oneself." When Daniel chose not to defile himself by eating the king's food and drinking the king's wine, he was making a public statement of personal consecration to his God. Daniel had consecrated himself in prayer. He practiced daily a two-way communication with God. With a consecrated prayer life comes assurance, faith and a holy boldness (courage). Daniel then requested that Ashpenaz put him and his three friends to the test. Daniel absolutely knew that God would honor their consecration to Him.

God is still looking for people today, both young and old, who will consecrate themselves to him. Believers who will separate themselves not from just sinful practices, but also from routines, relationships and ways that feed the flesh instead of the spirit. Admittedly, among the youth in the church today, such consecration is rare. Modern-day Daniels don't flock together. One or two might be found in a gathering of young believers. Even so, they are there, and the favor of God and men will be with them as they consecrate their lives to Him.

They Strengthened One Another

Daniel, Shadrach, Meshach and Abednego strengthened, encouraged, and built up one another. They shared much in common, but their strongest bond was their high standards based firmly on God's Word.

Parents with young children should pray that God would order the steps of their children to build relationships with other children who are devoted and consecrated to God. Youth usually become like the friends they associate with most frequently. As a parent, you may think you are helpless when it comes to the kinds of friends your children have in their teenage and later years. But you can begin to pray now! Pray specifically, and pray with a Spirit-led vision, that God will send your children friends who will "provoke" them to good works and holy living (see Hebrews 10:24).

I grew up in a church where as a youth I had many friends. Nevertheless, only one of my close friends strengthened me and inspired me to live a consecrated life in Christ. His name was Rod, and he happened to be the pastor's son. Even though my other friends and I would sometimes make fun of Rod or criticize him, we all respected him, because he had something we didn't have—the courage to possess standards.

Rod and I went to the same high school and were together a lot throughout our childhood and teen years. I loved being with Rod because he inspired and challenged me to devote my life to Christ. He never did it with words, but with his actions and attitudes. I don't think it's a coincidence that of all the friends I had in my teen years, he is the only sustaining friendship that still remains some 30 years later. Even now, when we get together, he still inspires me in my Christian journey. Hopefully, I inspire him as well.

I was blessed to have praying parents, a praying church family, and a praying grandmother who persevered day and night in prayer. God answered many of those prayers by sending me friends and loving family members to keep me built up and encouraged throughout my teen and college years. God will do the same for you and your children as you make it a priority in your prayer life.

They Loved Their God

We prove that we love God when we keep His commandments, according to 1 John 5:3. The four Hebrew boys showed they loved God with all their hearts, all their souls, and all their strength by choosing to obey God rather than pleasing man. As we have seen, they served and loved their pagan neighbors, while all along letting God's power and glory shine on their lives.

As Christian parents we often think in terms of teaching our children right from wrong rather than placing the greater emphasis on falling in love with God through a relationship with Jesus Christ. This is vital, because obedience flows naturally out of a loving relationship with God. This is why Jesus said that to "love the Lord thy God with all thy heart, and with all thy soul, and with all thy mind" is the first and great commandment, and that the second is loving your neighbor as yourself (Matthew 22:37-39). Jesus was saying that if we can get our vertical relationship with God right, then God gives us the capacity we need to get our horizontal relationships ordered right. Jesus summed it up by adding, "On these two commandments hang all the law and the prophets" (v. 40).

Jesus has always revealed, and is still revealing, who God the Father is and what He is doing. According to John 17:26, Jesus' purpose in doing this is so that the love of the Father for His Son might be in each of us. In other words, God wants His love in us so that we might be able to love Jesus like He loves Jesus, His Son. Now just slow down for a minute and digest that. God desires to put in us the same love that God the Father has for His Son, so that we can love Jesus with all of our heart, soul and mind.

Teach Discernment

In an article titled "Mind Over Media" on the *Focus on the Family* Webzine, the author writes, "Taking the time to teach discernment leads to critical thinking based on clearly defined criteria. It introduces scriptural principles (Philippians 4:8, Romans 12:2, Proverbs 4:24, Psalm 101:3). It unites families rather than divides them. It gives children life skills they can carry with them into adulthood. It requires time, energy, patience, open communication and earnest prayer to know how to navigate pop culture's 'gray areas.' But it is possible, and the rewards are great!"

To watch a video or a movie is a passive activity, but that doesn't mean that we are not affected by what we see and learn. My 12-year-old son can see a movie and weeks later describe in great detail certain scenes and quote line by line the actors in those scenes. What we see on the big screen has a powerful effect on people, especially kids. Vivid scenes linger, catchy melodies stick with us, funny phrases find their way into our everyday conversations with others. Certainly, images on television and movie screens powerfully influence our lives.

Many Christians have let their guard down when it comes to this form of amusement. They have become used to the swearing, the sex, the violence, the subtle (and sometimes not so subtle) anti-Christian messages found in many movies. They say—reasonably—that they want to be aware of the culture around them. But where do we draw the line between being in the world but not of it?

Taught or Caught?

A man in the Bible once gave some excellent advice on how to protect yourself and your family from the temptations of the flesh. Job said he made a solemn promise to himself never to look with lust at a woman (Job 31:1).

Several things strike me about Job's promise to himself:

• *His honesty.* The Bible says he was a worshiper of God and faithful to Him. It goes on to say, "He was a good man, careful not to do anything evil" (Job 1:1, *GNB*). But he hated evil, and he wanted to do what was right before God.

• *His humility.* Job knew himself; he realized that he was vulnerable to the temptations of the flesh. His worship and faithfulness was not just built upon the foundation of knowledge of God. Knowledge without humility "puffs up," or brings pride. Job had learned the practice of humbling himself before his God.

• *His self-discipline.* Job was determined to train his eyes to look away from sexy images, much like the way you jerk your hand away from a hot stove. Job made a vow, a solemn promise to himself. He disciplined himself to practice wholesomeness and purity as a lifestyle.

Habits are more easily caught than taught. Job was laying down some boundaries not only for himself but also for his sons and grandsons. Christian men, young or old, married or single, like Job, must make solemn pacts with God regarding their eyes. Sadly, many Christian men today choose to conveniently ignore the fact that sensual images have powerful influence. The reason is that sensual images bring visual sexual satisfaction. Most men, even Christian men, have convinced themselves that such habits are harmless to no one and sinless before God.

Nothing could be farther from the truth, Jesus said, "Anyone who looks at a woman and wants to possess her is guilty of committing adultery with her in his heart" (Matthew 5:28, *GNB).*

Furthermore, not only does God see it, but the children also observe and too often "catch it." Not everything that is caught by children is specifically taught to them. There are things in the spirit of a man or woman that can be passed on to the children through attitudes and behavior. This is why it is essential that Christian parents be filled with the Spirit of God. This way of life, this living in the Spirit, "produces love, joy, peace, patience, kindness, goodness, faithfulness, humility, and self-control" (Galatians 5:22, 23, *GNB*).

Would Shadrach, Meshach and Abednego have refused to bow before the golden image if they had not been taught the Word of God by their parents and teachers back in Judah? Do we expect our kids not to bow to today's image crafters without Christian parents who are radically committed to Christ and who impart His truths into their lives? Like Josiah's generation, we as 21st-century parents must rediscover the Word of God with a fresh conviction and passion. It must be both taught by the parents and caught by the children if they are to be prepared to face the fiery furnaces in their lives. We may not be able to go with them into their Babylons, but we can introduce them to the God who will be with them and live in them and give them overcoming power and grace.

DISCUSSION QUESTIONS

1. Discuss how Christianity in America has become its own subculture. What is the consequences of this for the church in America that is called by God to reach the lost?

2. Discuss ways that parents can pass on God's Word to their children in hopes of preparing them to live in a pagan world.

The Social Crafters

Chapter Four

"It's still hard to believe we don't all know, down deep, that abortion has not made our country a gentler place. I believe we haven't begun to appreciate the effect on our children and their developing understanding of life that they are told every day, on television and in magazines, in advertisements and news stories, that we allow the killing of children. It's not good for them to know that, not good for them to be told over and over that they live in a place where life is not necessarily respected and inconvenient life can be whisked away. Knowledge like that has a chilling effect on the soul."—Peggy Noonan, Wall Street Journal Editorial Page

For two consecutive years, the church I pastor performed a drama in which a variety of brief scenes were acted out during a 30-minute tour. Each scene depicted the possible consequences of certain permissible social practices like abortion, homosexuality, substance abuse (alcohol and drugs), sexual promiscuity and dabbling in the occult. Of the thousands of people who made these tours, approximately 80 percent of them were teens and young adults. In 23 years of pastoral ministry, I have never seen so many people physically, emotionally and spiritually shaken. After a reporter from the Cincinnati Enquirer completed the tour, she described it as "disturbing."

Why was it disturbing and troubling for so many people? For most, it was the painful reality of the lies that had been laid bare before their very eyes—lies told by the gay community, Planned Parenthood, sex educators, beer companies, tobacco producers and humanists, along with deceptions perpetuated by political, religious and corporate leaders, and the media. They hear lies like "It's not a life; its only a cell," "I can't help it that I'm gay; this is the way God made me," and false philosophies that say, "If it feels good, do it."

Consequently, millions of American adults have believed and bought the lies of the social crafters. The majority of these boast and celebrate their freedom and independence upon making their choice, when in reality they have surrendered themselves to captivity. What the thousands of people who walked through our church's dramatic scenes saw was the imprisonment and the destruction that the social crafters don't tell us about. Why would they want to. As Peggy Noonan writes, "Knowledge like this has a chilling effect on the soul."

HOMOSEXUALITY: *From Out of the Closet to In-Your-Face*

In 1986, in *Bowers vs. Hardwick*, a decision that lived in infamy among gays in America, the court had upheld a Georgia antisodomy law. At the time, 25 states had such laws. Some 17 years later, only four states banned sodomy between homosexuals.

In July 2003, the Supreme Court of the United States struck down the Texas antisodomy law by a 6-3 vote. The court's decision (in *Lawrence et al. v. Texas*) basically said that gays are entitled to respect for their private lives. In the words of Justice Anthony Kennedy, "The state cannot demean their existence or control by making their private sexual conduct a crime."

David Garrow, legal scholar at Emory University, called it "bigger than *Roe v. Wade*. " Sandy Rios, president of Concerned Women for America, predicted moral Armageddon, saying, "We're opening up a complete Pandora's box." Justice Antonin Scalia, who wrote the dissenting opinion, warned that the court's decision would undermine laws barring bigamy, incest and prostitution. He predicted that the court's decision would cause "a massive disruption of the current social order." If that rings true, what kind of societal change can we expect?

1. We can expect homosexuality to increase dramatically in America at an alarming rate among the Buster and Bridger generations. When a society's laws endorse homosexuality as an optional lifestyle, homosexual activity increases greatly. The British House of Lords in 1957 began to strike down England's laws barring homosexuality. In spite of homosexual leaders declaring publicly that relaxing the laws would not increase interest in it, the homosexual population has exploded in England since. The fact is, any society that approves such behavior will raise the curiosity level among children and teens, especially those who have gradually developed a predisposition toward it.

2. We can expect same-sex marriages to become legal in the United States. The laws barring such marriages now will certainly be challenged in the courts under the *Lawrence* decision.

3. We will see more gay couples adopting children. *Newsweek* magazine reports, "Already most states allow for single gays to adopt children."

4. We will see more custody of children battles to be won by homosexuals. Why? Because the court can no longer hold to the opinion that private sex between the opposite sex is immoral. Such reasoning will no longer factor in such cases.

5. We can expect more gay ministers serving as pastors and bishops in churches. In early August 2003, the Episcopal church for the most part was ecstatic over their decision to allow one of their pastors to serve in their church as a gay bishop. They even boasted that the rest of the churches in America would follow their lead as they have always done in the past.

6. You will also see more and more employers offer benefits to gay partners. Already, 197 of *Fortune*'s top 500 offer benefits to gay partners, including 27 of the top 50.

7. Pro-gay lawyers will now have more leverage concerning gay discrimination laws because of the *Lawrence* case. Organizations like Big Brothers saw this coming when it recently enacted policy forcing all 490 of its local chapters around the country to accept

homosexuals as mentors. How can pairing a boy starving for male attention with a homosexual man be a good idea—especially when many mainstream gay leaders continue to promote the virtues of sex between men and boys? The *San Francisco Sentinel* stated: "The love between men and boys is at the foundation of homosexuality." Another gay publication, *The Guide*, declared: "Instead of fearing being labeled pedophiles, we must proudly proclaim that sex is good, including children's sexuality. We must do it for the children's sake."

'We Are Just Like Everyone Else'

Groups such as the Lambda Legal Defense and Education Fund are trying to soften up public opinion with town hall meetings designed to show that gay families are good for the community. In the town hall meetings, people like Cindy Meneghin, who partners with Maureen and has two children, testify, "Hey, we're just like anyone else. . . . You cannot look at our beautiful, charming kids and not notice that we're a family, and the myths start tumbling down."

The Lambda Defense Fund is not the only organization trying to soften public opinion. American television networks have joined the effort as well with an unabashed in-your-face progay campaign.

Robert Bianco, of *USA Today*, called 2003 a landmark year for gay people on TV, which saw "gay themes, characters and people advance on all TV fronts." Network and cable television premiered gay programs such as *Boy Meets Boy*, *Queer Eye for the Straight Guy*, *It's All Relative*, *A Minute With Stan Hooper*, as well as gay-oriented movies and shows.

The prevailing trend currently preoccupying magazines and afternoon talk shows, and no doubt coming soon to prime-time TV, is young women who experiment with bisexuality for a sense of empowerment and as a way to seduce men. Alessandra Stanley, in a *New York Times* article, "Women Having Sex, Hoping Men Tune In," calls the Showtime series *The L Word* "a manifesto of lesbian liberation and visual candy for men."

Stanley, in her *TV Weekend* review, wrote, "While ostensibly celebrating the lesbian life, the two-hour pilot [*The L Word*] is in such a rush to pander to male viewers that at times it seems less like an American television show than a hastily dubbed Swedish 'art' film. Each new plot development works as a perfunctory excuse to introduce another sexual variation—a man alone, a man with a woman, two women, two women and a man, etc."

What Is the Truth?

The facts show that homosexual relationships are not normal. Homosexuals are not like everyone else, and they do not make beautiful, cohesive families that contribute to society as a whole. Furthermore, there is absolutely no scientific evidence that homosexuality is genetic, as some gay activist groups would lead us to believe.

Even gay researchers don't dispute this. Dr. Simon LeVay, the neuroscientist who studied the hypothalamus in gay men, told *Discover* magazine, "I did not prove that homosexuality is genetic, or find a genetic cause for being gay. I didn't show that gay men are born that way, the most common mistake people make in interpreting my work."

A recently released Dutch study shows that the average homosexual relationship lasts only one and a half years. Even those within a so-called committed gay relationship have an average of eight partners a year. According to Mike Haley, a former homosexual who is a staff member at Focus on the Family, research consistently finds gay relationships to be transitory and promiscuous.

Mr. Haley says that gay men are looking for love in all the wrong places. He states, "When you're taking an unmet emotional need that's being met in a sexual way, that sexual need will never meet the emotional need, and that's why we see these relationships falling apart over and over again."

Ex-gays like Haley are troubled by gay activists' claims that homosexuals live "normal, healthy lives." They know that gay men are 1,000 times more likely to contract AIDS than the general population and that their life expectancy is cut by up to 20 years. They also cite a 2001 report in the *Journal of the American Medical Association* that indicates gays and lesbians have extremely high rates of psychiatric illness, drug and alcohol abuse, and suicide. Gay groups argue that these problems are caused by our "homophobic society." But the research reported in the AMA journal was conducted in the Netherlands, which is arguably one of the gay-friendliest countries on earth.

Are homosexual families normal, average families? Recently, the son of a homosexual man wrote an article that appeared on the *Boundless Webzine,* called "My Father's Closet."

"After my parents' separation, my sister and I began spending every other weekend with my father in the city. He shared a condo with a man who had also left his wife and children. The man's two daughters seemed to have adjusted to the situation. It was as if everything was 'normal.' But I felt anything but normal. It was as if I had fallen asleep and woken up in a bizarre alternate reality. At the end of the day, my father would not walk into the bedroom with my mom, like he had done only weeks before. Instead, he headed off to bed with a man I had met only days before.

Those weekends were a nightmare for my sister and me. Not only were we forced to leave our mother and friends, but we were placed in a culture we knew nothing about. It was not just a foreign culture; it was one which was anathema to the community in which we were raised. We had gone from the Garden of Eden to Sodom and Gomorrah. How could my father, who once reigned over our Eden, suddenly become a supporter of what we had seen as the enemy?"

What's obvious is that today's youth generation is receiving all kinds of mythical, confusing, and misleading information from the social crafters. Deception and lies abound, and it seems as if the truth is being deliberately hidden. The stakes have never been higher, with the institution of marriage, family and, as Justice Scalia warned, "our current social order"—all could be up for grabs. If there ever was a time for a people committed to the truth about homosexuality to pass it on to today's youth culture, it is now. If God's people don't stand up and stand firm on the Word of God, not in a spirit of condemnation, but in the spirit of God's love, the social crafters will keep the truth hidden from present and future generations.

Randy L. Ballard

ABORTION: The Crafting of Infant Death

I was 13 years old when *Roe v. Wade* opened the door to abortion on demand in America. I don't remember an outcry from the church or the community. I can't recall that it was even mentioned in the pulpit or the church where we attended. I don't remember discussions of it in any of my classes in junior high and high school. I don't think it was an issue that was a part of the public discourse in the '70s.

Where was the outrage when the *Roe* ruling came down? Back then (before Watergate), people pretty much trusted their government, especially the stately men in the black robes at the Supreme Court. The media wasn't as vast and advanced as it is today, and far less skeptical in those days. Our culture as a whole, especially Christians, seemed somewhat blindsided by the *Roe* decision. One reason for this was that the court broke the rules of American government, stealing the issue from the legislative branch. Instead of interpreting the Constitution, the court wrote a new law. Think of it as a basketball game in which the referee takes the ball and scores several points for one team—the team that gets the points is ecstatic; the team that doesn't can't believe what they just saw with their own eyes.

It is clearly understandable why the opponents of abortion have battled with the unfairness and the frustration of the Court's decision for over 30 years now. The ruling has become one of the most important decisions in the history of the Supreme Court. With this right protected by the Court, people can legally kill babies in the womb. Even though the Supreme Court with its decision may have been trying to save the country from a messy debate, *Roe* has divided us as a people and has inflamed the debate even more.

Products of Conception?

C. Everett Koop, former surgeon general of the United States, wrote, "We who as a people always knew that abortion was the killing of the unborn baby were brainwashed to believe that the destruction of the 'products of conception' or the destruction of a 'fetus is not the same thing as killing an unborn baby. Traditional medical definitions were deliberately changed in order to do away with our moral repugnance toward abortion."

The proabortionists referred to the abortion process as "interrupting" rather than terminating a pregnancy. They spoke of "evacuating the contents of the uterus" or of removing "postconceptive fertility content." They referred to the unborn baby as "potential human life," when it is obvious the organism is human and alive before birth.

It wasn't until Jerry Falwell's Moral Majority in the early '80s that the evangelical church in America began to acknowledge what had happened in *Roe v. Wade*. By then, the sexual revolution was in full bloom and abortions were becoming common on college campuses and elsewhere. While the evangelical church in America was waking up out of its isolating snooze, it is estimated that over 10 million babies had been aborted during *Roe's* first decade of existence.

Today, the generally accepted number of abortions that have been performed since the 1973 ruling is 40 million. That's 40 million children banished from life. Peggy Noonan writes, "Forty million. There isn't a country in the world with an army that big. Many don't have a population that big. . . . It seems realistic to assume the 40 million would have included your average mix of heroes, villains and those undistinguished by recognizable gifts. But actually I wonder about that. It has seemed to me over the years that so many of the 40 million were the children of bright or educated or affluent parents, lucky young people and, in the way of things, might likely have gone on to . . . well, we might have lost more curers of cancer than we know. In any case, whatever these individuals would have become, they were all unique, blessed. They all deserved the same thing, life, and all suffered the same fate."

Most opinion polls today say that the majority of Americans believe that abortion should be illegal in the United States. It's a no-brainer in the scientific community that life begins at fertilization. In the summer of 2003, a motion was filed to reopen and overturn *Roe v. Wade*, brought by the one person who can do so—the "Jane Roe" of *Roe v. Wade*, Norma McCorvey. When we consider that opinion polls, medical science, and even the author of *Roe v. Wade* favor life over abortion, why are we still in the abortion business? The answer: Abortion is big business, a multimillion-dollar-a-year business.

Planned Parenthood's Fat Coffers

In 2003, Planned Parenthood turned a profit to the tune of $36 million, which is a threefold increase over the previous year's profits. Planned Parenthood is a federally funded agency with an annual budget of $450 million and a work force of 22,000 people. "Across the United States, the abortion rates are still falling, and yet at Planned Parenthood it went up from 213,000 [in 2002] to 227,385 [in 2003]," said Jim Sedlak, executive director of the pro-life group Stop Planned Parenthood.

Other 2003 data released by Planned Parenthood revealed that the group referred fewer than 2,000 women to adoption agencies and that U.S. taxpayers gave more than $250 million to the nonprofit organization—roughly a third of its total income. Donors might think they are giving to an organization dedicated to "family planning." But "family planning" is only a euphemism for abortion.

"Planned Parenthood's plans typically don't include parenthood," explained Sedlak. "They're not prepared for it. They talk about being for choice, but they really don't offer women much of a choice."

Baby Parts for Sale

There's another dirty business that no one likes to talk about— the sale of baby parts which is big business in North America. The National Institutes of Health Revitalization Act of 1993 made it a federal felony for any person to "knowingly, for 'valuable consideration,' purchase or sell the organs and bodies of aborted children."

But fetal-tissue brokers, the middlemen between abortion clinics and researchers, have schemes to circumvent the law (if they don't break it outright), and they know how to deceive couriers so that a package of dead babies ships more easily than a carton of cigarettes.

The U.S. House of Representatives on November 9, 2003, approved by voice vote a "Sense of Congress Resolution" (H.R. 350) calling for "hearings concerning private companies that are involved in the trafficking of baby body parts."

On the House floor, Representative Tom Tancredo read from a fetal-tissue broker price list: "$50 for eyes, $150 for lungs and hearts, and $999 for an eight-week brain." The price list read by Tancredo is one of about 50 forms obtained by Life Dynamics, Inc., a Denton, Texas-based pro-life group known for its renegade tactics and for recruiting "spies" in the abortion industry.

Life Dynamics was approached about two years ago by an abortion-clinic insider who uses the pseudonym "Kelly" because she reportedly fears for her life. Kelly at the time was working for a Maryland-based private firm called the Anatomic Gift Foundation (AGF). She said her job was to procure fetal tissue for research. When babies started arriving alive for dissection, she went to Life Dynamics.

Kelly quit her job and provided Life Dynamics with fetal-tissue order forms from researchers throughout North America, plus commercial price lists for babies and baby parts from two private companies that act as brokers between abortion clinics and researchers. Kelly's following testimony provides the gruesome details of daily work for AGF:

"We would get a generated list each day to tell us what tissue researchers, pharmaceuticals and universities were looking for. Then we would go and look at the particular patient charts—we had to screen out anyone who had STDs [sexually transmitted diseases] or fetal anomalies. These had to be the most perfect specimens we could give these researchers for the best value that we could sell for." Only about 10 percent of fetuses were ruled out, she said. The rest were "healthy donors."

"Donors" ranged in age from seven weeks to full term. Kelly said she harvested tissue from 30 to 40 "late" fetuses each week. She said the clinic routinely used the partial-birth-abortion technique wherein the baby's entire body is delivered feet first and face down, the surgeon punctures the base of the baby's skull, inserts a cannula to suck out the brain matter, then slides the head out.

Sometimes, the three-day process that prepared the women for the abortion procedure had alarming complications. Beforehand, the patients were inserted with laminaria—typically seaweed—which dilates the cervix, and in several cases, the women went into labor.

"[The babies] were coming out alive," said Kelly, who recalled three or four live births in a typical two-week period.

Kelly said in a videotaped interview with Life Dynamics that the doctors "would either break the neck or take a pair of tongs and basically beat the fetus until it was dead."

On another occasion, a doctor presented Kelly with perfectly formed 24-week-old twins, moving and gasping for air in a steel pan. When Kelly objected, she said, she watched the doctor fill the pan with water until it ran over the babies' mouths and noses.

"That's when I decided it was wrong," she said.

What Does God Think?

You may be thinking, *I can't believe this kind of stuff really goes on.* But in the real world, it happens every day. However, in the real medical world, *Roe* is growing further and further out of date. Now babies are able to survive outside the womb in the second trimester. The Supreme Court said in 1973 that it could not interfere with a woman's right to abortion during the first two trimesters because the baby was not viable during that time. Today, we have multitudes of humans walking around as "viable evidence," who can testify to the Court's erroneous judgment.

We Americans like to think of ourselves as tenderhearted, giving and compassionate. Nonetheless, *Roe v. Wade* has hardened us as a people. We do our best to ignore its consequences. We try to soften the rhetoric by saying that as a whole we are better than this—that the abortionist, the baby-parts dealers, are the real bad guys. But it only takes a little leaven to leaven the whole; and *Roe v. Wade* was the little leaven that has defiled us as a nation.

There are many who think that God somehow overlooks the 40 million babies murdered, that He weighs all the good we do and at the end of the day still rains down His blessings upon us. But the God of the Bible does not ignore sin, especially the sin of destroying so many young, innocent lives. Our excuses and our justifications don't change His commandments. He still says, "Thou shall not kill." The psalmist wrote, "But when you give them breath, they are created" (Psalm 104:30, *GNB*). He gives life, and only He has the authority to take life.

God instructed Moses to set a law before the children of Israel that clearly brings the sanctity of life of unborn children into focus: "If men who are fighting hit a pregnant woman and she gives birth prematurely but there is not serious injury, the offender must be fined whatever the woman's husband demands and the court allows. But if there is serious injury, you are to take life for life, eye for eye, tooth for tooth, hand for hand, foot for foot" (Exodus 21:22-24, *NIV*).

John Calvin makes a significant observation concerning abortion in commenting on the Exodus passage: "The fetus, though in the womb of his mother, is already a human being, and it is a monstrous crime to rob it of life which it has not yet begun to enjoy. If it seems more horrible to kill a man in his house than in a field, because a man's house is his place of most secure refuge, it ought surely to be deemed more atrocious to destroy a fetus in the womb before it has come to light."

After the children of Israel settled in the Promised Land, Israel ignored God's law and began offering up their children to the god of fire, whom they called Molech. Much like we in America think today, Israel thought that because God's blessing and prosperity were upon their nation, they could get away with murder. We should learn from Israel's history. We should heed the warning of the prophet Jeremiah before it's too late: "Just as a hunter fills a cage with birds, they have filled their houses with loot. That is why they are powerful and rich, why they are fat and well fed. There is no limit to their evil deeds. They do not give orphans their rights or show justice to the oppressed. But I, the Lord, will punish them for these things; I will take revenge on this nation. A terrible and shocking thing has happened in the land: prophets speak nothing but lies; priests rule as the prophets command, and my people offer no objections. But what will they do when it all comes to an end?" (5:27-31, *GNB*).

SEX EDUCATION: Break the Condoms or Wait for the Vows?

Another area that today's social crafters have targeted is teenage sexual education. In many schools, young people are provided with all the physical facts on sexuality, including detailed information about contraception and, in some cases, presentations of homosexuality and other behaviors labeled "alternative lifestyles." With the rampant spread of adolescent pregnancy and sexually transmitted diseases (STDs), more schools are making the discussion of human sexuality a part of their curriculum. The trouble is that instruction on such an issue can produce undesirable results. While parts of this curriculum can be educational and helpful, other parts can be nothing more than the introduction of alternative sexual values that have unhealthy consequences for your child.

What Is "Mature Teen Sex"?

What a bizarre, oxymoronic concept—teens practicing "mature teen sex." Believe it or not, this is the latest "solution" to the teenage sexuality problem from our culture's most educated minds: If we can't keep teens from having sex, then we should try to teach them to have "responsible" and "mature sex." That's like trying to turn a hog in the pigpen into Miss Piggy, the muppet. But Miss Piggy is not real; she is a fantasy character—just as teens having mature, responsible sex is not reality.

Recently, SIECUS (Sexuality Information and Education Council of the United States) compiled a report for U.S. legislators that offers the failed values-neutral philosophy of the '60s in modern rhetoric. SIECUS tells us that "responsible" teen sex should be "consensual, nonexploitive, honest, pleasurable and protected." They make no mention of love and little to commitment. The report stresses that sexual behavior consists of a host of physical acts ranging from touching to various kinds of intercourse. Additionally, they recognize that these behaviors may take place with a same-sex partner! The document makes 344 references to sex, two references to commitment, and none to spiritual beliefs and values. The organization's goal is to indoctrinate our children with this philosophy from preschool to 12th grade.

Safe Sex vs. Abstinence

Why is it that public education maintains that teen pregnancy and STDs are the issue, while ignoring that teens simply engaging in sex is the real problem? During the '80s and '90s, "Why Wait?" youth campaigns in churches encouraged hundreds of thousands of teens to wait until marriage to have sex. The media couldn't believe it. They asked . . . how could we expect teens to wait until marriage—hadn't we heard that vows break easier than condoms? The media and much of public education viewed such programs as unrealistic and labeled it from the far right.

But the real worry of the "safe sex" campaigners is that if abstinence education is allowed to succeed, their livelihood is in jeopardy. Many safe-sex promoters have attempted to take over the process, trying to cut out abstinence-until-marriage groups completely. Durex condoms mounted a campaign against abstinence called "Truth for Youth." Durex's spokesperson claimed that abstinence until marriage would move the nation "backward" in reducing teen pregnancy. Durex met with politicians, health educators and school officials to reach kids with the safe-sex message. Ironically, Durex had its hand slapped by the Federal Trade Commission for deceptive advertising and by the Food and Drug Administration for defective condoms. So much for "truth for youth."

Nonetheless, youth are beginning to learn the truth about abstinence. In 1996, Congress allotted $250 million over five years to give abstinence-only education the same voice that safe-sex advocates have enjoyed for the past 20 years—with your tax dollars! The abstinence program created by the welfare law established that the only acceptable standard of sexual activity in our nation is abstinence until marriage. The program was bold, visionary and unapologetic, and by all indications the national abstinence program is producing positive results. Teen pregnancy, abortion and birth rates are falling, and teen birth rates are now at their lowest levels in decades.

The battle for teen sexual purity for our nation is a victory worth fighting for. Parents, teens, pastors, teachers and Christians everywhere must continue to speak up for abstinence. The divorce and teen-pregnancy rate in the church is equal to that in secular society, so more than ever the church needs to preach, teach and model holiness and purity. Parents must practice open, honest communication with their children, especially through their teen years. The world has failed our children by treating sex education as a "class" where you get your information and then go out to "pass" or "fail." Rather, sex education should be a continuous dialogue from youth to adulthood and into marriage.

SUBSTANCE ABUSE: The Plague of Youth Culture

The consumption of alcohol, tobacco and addicting drugs has become a modern-day plague sweeping through cities, small towns, schools and families. Substance abuse is a respecter of no one; it lures its victims without regard to racial, geographic, family, economic, religious or educational boundaries. Most recently, preteens, and even elementary-age children, have been drawn into using drugs. Why has substance abuse become so attractive to the youth culture in the last 35 years? What are the social factors that have led to this epidemic among youth in America?

The Sex-Appeal Factor

Smoking and drinking are widely promoted in pop culture as habits enjoyed by sophisticated, fun-loving, attractive, sexy people—what most adolescents long to become. Beer commercials use high-profile rock stars, athletes and scantily dressed models to imply to youth that they are not cool unless they drink their brand of beer. It's bad enough for youth to have their peers pressuring them to drink and smoke, but then when the media promotes it in commercials, movies and music videos, it proves to be too much social reinforcement for many youth to withstand.

The Home Factor

Children learn what they live. When parents smoke, usually their kids smoke. When parents use drugs and alcohol, usually their kids will too. The drug experimenters of the '60s and '70s are the parents of today's teens and young adults. Today's youth have grown up in a drug culture. They have a greater familiarity and knowledge of drugs than their parents. They have a greater variety of drugs to choose from. With substance usage on the rise, undoubtedly the generational sins of the fathers have come upon their sons and daughters.

The Peer-Pressure Factor

Peers play a huge role at each stage of a child's or adolescent's drug experience—whether resisting them, experimenting, becoming a user, or confronting withdrawal and recovery. The need for peer acceptance is especially strong during the early adolescent years and can override (or at least seriously challenge) the most earnest commitments. "Just say no" may not mean much when smoking, drinking or taking drugs determines who is included in highly esteemed ranks of the inner circle.

The Escape Factor

If everyday life seems boring, meaningless, oppressive or painful (physically and/or emotionally), alcohol and drugs may appear to offer a powerful time-out. This is often the driving force in drug use. The strongest resistance to drug abuse, therefore, arises from an ongoing sense of joy and contentment that transcends circumstances. These attitudes are usually acquired, not inborn. Early positive experiences in the family and an active, wide-awake relationship with God play the most important roles in molding such attitudes.

POLITICAL CORRECTNESS AND TOLERANCE: The Erasing of the Lines

Whether it's the gay community, television, education, music or pop culture in general, as Dr. Dobson stated, if they gain control of the children, they can change the entire culture in one generation. The ideas and agendas of today's social crafters consist of nothing new or fresh. What has changed drastically is the social landscape of our culture. Never before have young minds been so open to influences outside traditional lines, simply because so many lines have been erased.

Today's youth are a generation removed from a society guided by Judeo-Christian ethics and have been raised on a daily diet of moral relativism since birth. Most of today's college students have grown up believing that there are no absolute standards that apply to everybody in all situations. The word *truth* now means "true for me." In other words, truth is subjective and based on internal preferences. In contrast, objective truths are those things learned in the external realm that cannot be changed by how we feel.

Allan Bloom wrote, "There is one thing a professor can be absolutely certain of: Almost every student entering the university believes, or says he believes, that truth is relative. If this belief is put to the test, one can count on the students' reaction: They will be uncomprehending. That anyone should regard the proposition as not self-evident astonishes them, as though he were calling into question 2+2=4."

When objective truth no longer exists in the minds of people, subjective personal opinion is all that remains. Public opinion polls become the voice of virtue. Without belief in absolute truths, the idea of moral truths becomes irrational. Morality is reduced to what one thinks is best "for me" or "what feels good."

Relativists charge with "intolerance" those that do adhere to standards they believe to be absolute. Moral relativism says there are no standards that determine what is right or wrong. Consequently, judgment and discretion are rejected for fear of being found guilty of judgmentalism and discrimination. Such individuals are often labeled in a "politically correct" society as narrow-minded, mean and insensitive.

Kay Haugaard teaches creative writing at Pasadena City College and says she has for more than 20 years been teaching "The Lottery," Shirley Jackson's short story in which the citizens of a small town ritually stone one of their number to death. Jackson's story used to shock people into moral judgment. No longer, according to Ms. Haugaard. After a lengthy discussion, it became apparent that her students thought they were in no position to judge people who followed different traditions.

"At this point I gave up. No one in the whole class of more than twenty ostensibly intelligent individuals would go out on a limb and take a stand against human sacrifice."

Robert L. Simon, a professor of philosophy at Hamilton College in Clinton, New York, writes that whatever else students may dare to do, they will not risk being thought of as moral absolutists: "I have yet to meet even one student who has expressed doubts about whether the Holocaust actually happened. However, I have recently seen an increasing number of students who, although well-meaning, hold almost as troubling a view. They accept the reality of the Holocaust, but they believe themselves unable morally to condemn it, or indeed to make any moral judgments whatsoever.

Such students typically comment that they themselves deplore the Holocaust and other great evils, but then they wind up by suspending moral judgment. . . . By denying themselves the moral authority to condemn such great evils of human history as the Holocaust, slavery and racial oppression, these students lose the basis for morally condemning wrongdoing anywhere. . . . Then the truly arrogant and truly fanatical need not fear moral censure no matter what evil they choose to inflict on us all."

Modern culture crafters have done their job well by indoctrinating today's students with one of the key virtues of moral relativism: the principle of tolerance. Tolerance means "I ought to tolerate the moral opinions and behavior of others who disagree with me. I should not try to interfere with their opinions or behavior."

This is the kind of world that moral relativism produces: Nothing is evil or good, nothing is right or wrong, and everything is subject to one's own personal ethics, that is, what is "truth for me." If living today, Dr. Francis Schaeffer would probably assert in regards to relativists that they "have both feet firmly planted in midair."

Randy L. Ballard

What About Today's Christian Youth?

What effect does pop culture have on today's Christian young people? Tens of thousands of youth in America attend Christian music concerts and buy CDs. They wear T-shirts with Christian messages, along with WWJD (What Would Jesus Do?) bracelets, but according to Josh McDowell, a leading authority regarding Christian youth culture, "Many of them are defining God in their own way."

According to the Barna studies, 72 percent of Christian teens believe that "you can tell if something is morally and ethically right for you by whether or not it works in your life."

"Consequently, our kids feel no need to discuss such abstract ideas as the absolute truths of God's Word; they see little reason to grapple with what they believe about Christ and why. "What's the point?" they would most likely say. "As long as it works for me, that's all I care about." McDowell sees kids today using Scripture merely as a springboard for thought as they attempt to create their own personal "meaning," one that may have little or nothing to do with the objective meaning of the Biblical text.

Is the idea "If it's right for me, it will work" practical in the real world? Hardly, both God's Word and life experiences teach us that you can do what's right and it still may not always "work out." The Bible records the story of Job, who was a "perfect and upright man, and one that feared God" (Job 1:1). But after a long period of prosperity in Job's life, he suffered a number of major setbacks and disasters. My wife, Annette, has a close, intimate relationship with Jesus Christ, but in 1997 she was diagnosed with Hodgkin's disease (a form of cancer), followed by almost a year of chemotherapy and radiation treatments.

Research studies and observation have shown that kids are biologically wired for intimate relationship. Anyone who has ever been a parent knows that. If parents will model and teach Christlike values to their children, the children will learn that a close relationship with Jesus Christ, based in the truth of the Scriptures, will provide the framework needed to define God as His Spirit guides them.

Objective truth is not enough. Kids need to see truth "fleshed out" in the lives of parents and others with whom they are bonded in relationship.

RELIGIOUS EXPRESSION: The Assault Upon Our Foundations

For decades, members of the U.S. Supreme Court openly embraced our nations Biblical foundations. In an 1892 decision, the Court stated, "Our laws and our institutions must necessarily be based upon and embody the teachings of the Redeemer of mankind. It is impossible that it should be otherwise; and in this sense and to this extent our civilization and our institutions are emphatically Christian. This is a religious people. This is historically true. . . . This is a Christian nation" (*Church of the Holy Trinity v. United States*, 1892).

President Calvin Coolidge acknowledged, "The foundations of our society and our government rest so much on the teachings of the Bible that it would be difficult to support them if faith in these teachings would cease to be practically universal in our country." Coolidge understood that if the foundations are destroyed, our nation won't just cease to be moral, it could very well cease being a nation at all.

The two quotes above came from the Supreme Court and a former U.S. president who recognized that the framers of the Constitution believed that religious freedom was supremely important. Any true study of colonial history shows that the primary reason English settlers came to America was for *freedom of religion,* not *freedom from religion.*

The assurance of religious liberty was the very intent of the two separation clauses placed back to back in the First Amendment of the Constitution known as the "Establishment Clause" and the "Free Exercise Clause." The Establishment Clause states: "Congress shall make no law respecting an establishment of religion. . . ." The "Free Exercise Clause" reads, "...or prohibiting the free exercise thereof."

America's forefathers adopted the separation clauses for the clear purpose of promoting religious freedoms. Most Americans today have been indoctrinated with the idea that the First Amendment contains language requiring a wall of separation between church and state, when, in reality, such language cannot be found anywhere in the Constitution, Declaration of Independence, Bill of Rights or the Federalist Papers. The language of a wall of separation between church and state was taken from a letter penned by Thomas Jefferson several years after the Constitution was written. Sadly, Jefferson's phrase has been distorted and taken out of context by those advocating a rigid separation between church and state.

Supreme Court Justice Hugo Black, in his majority opinion in *Everson v. Board of Education* (1947), became the first justice to incorporate—out of context, many would argue—Jefferson's "wall of separation" language into American jurisprudence. "The First Amendment, " said Black, "has erected a wall between church and state. That wall must be kept high and impregnable. We could not approve the slightest breach." Justice Black gave the separation language its first teeth, delineating its initial parameters.

Justice Hugo Black's majority opinion has served as the cornerstone piece for the growing, rampant anti-Christian discrimination conducted by modern-day social crafters. Increasingly, Hollywood, the mainstream media, and those who adhere to the PC (political correctness) codes are targeting Christians. In David Limbaugh's eye-opening book *Persecution*, he reveals hundreds of true stories of Christians in America who are increasingly being driven from public life, denied First Amendment rights, and even actively discriminated against for their beliefs. Limbaugh tells of social crafters who not only prohibit school prayer and forbid students from wearing Christian symbols, like a simple cross, but even expunge the real story of Christianity in America from history textbooks. Limbaugh reminds us that tolerance might be the highest virtue in pop culture, but it doesn't often extend to Christians these days.

The Truth: Offensive or Liberating?

A newspaper reporter once asked me why the Cincinnati gay and lesbian community was so upset about our church stating publicly that homosexuality was a sin and if a homosexual did not repent they would spend eternity in hell. My answer was brief and to the point: "The truth is offensive to those who would rather believe a lie."

The fact is, millions of Americans have believed and bought the lies of today's social crafters, including many who call themselves Christians. The prophet Jeremiah wrote, "They are always ready to tell lies; dishonesty instead of truth rules the land. The Lord says, 'My people do one evil thing after another and do not acknowledge me as their God' (Jeremiah 9:3, *GNB).*

The Bible best describes today's social crafters in Job 13:4: "You cover up your ignorance with lies; you are like doctors who can't heal anyone" (*GNB*). Job says the problem with lies is *they can't heal anyone.* Believing and living a lie leaves people empty, worthless and wounded. This is where American pop culture is today. We have bought into the deceitful lies of the secular humanists in the 20th century, and the end result is a generation without meaning or purpose and who are alienated from our Creator.

In sharp contrast, the truth of the gospel of Jesus Christ liberates. Jesus said, "I am the way, the truth, and the life; no one goes to the Father except by me" (John 14:6, *GNB).* Only Christ sets individuals, families, communities and nations free from the guilt and power of sins such as homosexuality, abortion, adultery, drugs, alcohol, and foolish philosophies and ideas. In the end, it is the truth as revealed in Christ that social crafters are trying to suppress. If they succeed, Coolidge's warning will become a fulfilled prophecy. We will cease to be moral, and we will cease to be a nation.

America's Most Coveted Commodity

In his recent book, David Aikman, a former *Time* magazine Beijing bureau chief, begins the first chapter by quoting a scholar from the Chinese Academy of Social Sciences (CASS), one of China's premier academic research institutes. This particular scholar was the evening guest lecturer speaking to a group of American tourists as they were concluding a long day of touring Beijing.

"One of the things we were asked to look into was what accounted for the success, in fact, the preeminence of the West all over the world," he said. "We studied everything we could from the historical, political, economic and cultural perspective. At first, we thought it was because you had more powerful guns than we had. Then we thought it was because you had the best political system. Next we focused on your economic system. But in the past twenty years, we have realized that the heart of your culture is your religion: Christianity. That is why the West has been so powerful. The Christian moral foundation of social and cultural life was what made possible the emergence of capitalism and then the successful transition to democratic politics. We don't have any doubt about this."

The apostle Paul wrote, "For God has already placed Jesus Christ as the one and only foundation, and no other foundation can be laid" (1 Corinthians 3:11,*GNB*).

DISCUSSION QUESTIONS

1. Discuss how the legalization of abortion has effected our culture as a whole in the last 30 years.

2. Should the church take a stronger stand against abortion? If so, what can the church do?

3. What can parents do today to protect children from substance abuse?

4. Discuss the connection between America's moral foundation and the success of capitalism in America.

Countering the Social Crafters:
Building Security and Stability

Chapter Five

The following excerpt was taken from an NBC Today interview with Nicole Nowlen, one of the survivors of the shooting at Columbine High School.

Interviewer: *"Do you remember much from the horrible day, April 20, 1999?"*

Nicole: *"Yes, I remember a lot. I could talk with your for two hours about it. People are surprised how much I remember, but I remember it all. I mean, how could I forget? I was in the library when Eric and Dylan came in shooting. I was in the wrong place at the wrong time. They came up to the table where we were sitting and they shot us . . ."* Her voice trailed off as she brought the scene to her memory. Her lip quivered, *"I was shot nine times in the stomach."*

Interviewer: *"How are you doing now? I mean, you look like you've completely recovered."*

Nicole: *"I'm doing well. I don't have problems like some people, like not being able to sleep and other problems."*

Interviewer: *"You're doing well physically. How are you emotionally?"*

Nicole: *"I am doing well. Of course, I won't really know until I go to school tomorrow. That's the first day of school. It might be scary being back at Columbine."*
Interviewer: *"What will be different?"*
Nicole: *"I'm different now. I'm no longer innocent and naïve. I liked it better when I was."*

When I think about the culture today with its myriad of social tentacles reaching out to snatch and devour my preteen son, I sometimes have thoughts of confining him to his room until he's 21. I am kidding, of course, but as a parent I do wish that Planet Earth was a kinder, gentler place for him. At times, I wish that the *Mayberry* and *Leave It to Beaver* kind of world still exists . . . and it does to some extent for the naïve and the innocent. But most of us are like Nicole, we have learned that innocence doesn't guarantee safety and security. And also, like Nicole, we realize that we are different now.

So how do we counter the 21st-century social crafters? Is there anything we can do as parents, teachers and leaders to prevent today's youth from being defiled by the social ills of our day? How do we prepare our children for the real world?

A Cry for Security and Stability

One thing we must realize is that today's youth want to live safe, predictable and secure lives. They may act cool and confident, but they are all seeking stability and security in a changing world. We live in uncertain times. Eighty-seven percent of the adults surveyed in a CNN/Gallup poll taken shortly after the 9/11 attacks reported, "September 11 is the most tragic event of my life." Such an event was shocking, unexpected, on U.S. soil! It all adds up to the same question our teens are asking: "Where can I be safe?"

You may wonder what security has to do with homosexuality, abortion, teen sexuality, political correctness, drugs and alcohol. The answer is *everything.* Social ills often lead to unstable and insecure homes and lives. As a pastor and a counselor for nearly 25 years, I have pastored children with homosexual parents. I have cried and prayed with them through their times of pain and confusion.

I have counseled with women in their 40s and 50s who were still struggling with an abortion that occurred 20 years earlier. I have collected offerings for and taken food to children with parents who drink, snort cocaine, or gamble their paychecks away. I have taken fatherless teenage boys fishing with me—boys who were fatherless because they are the result of a teenage pregnancy that occurred when the mothers relented, sometimes for the first time in their lives, to the pressure of their boyfriends for sex. It's not at all irrational or foolish to equate today's social sins with the cries for security and stability of today's youth.

The Need for Standards and Boundaries

Proverbs 19:18 says, "Chasten thy son while there is hope, and let not thy soul spare for his crying." The word *chasten* means "to instruct, teach or reprove." More than ever, children today need strong standards and boundaries. They need to know what is expected of them. Such instruction must begin in the home in their early-infancy years.

The New York research organization Public Agenda surveyed adults and concluded, "Americans are convinced that today's adolescents face a crisis—not in their economic or physical well-being but in their values and morals." Nine out of 10 adults said that the failure to learn values is widespread, and only 19 percent said that parents are commonly good role models. The Public Agenda study suggests that children are not the only ones who need limits on their behavior.

David, one of history's greatest kings and leaders understood where personal values and morals come from. He wrote, "I have avoided all evil conduct, because I want to obey your word. I have not neglected your instructions, because you yourself are my teacher. How sweet is the taste of your instructions—sweeter even than honey! I gain wisdom from your laws, and so I hate all bad conduct" (Psalm 119:101-104, *GNB*).

In these passages, David professes that God's Spirit is his teacher and because he has a close, intimate relationship with God, he hates evil conduct and chooses to avoid it. True security and stability in the 21st century doesn't come from metal detectors or the National Homeland Security Department. Our children's security isn't going to come from a school values-clarification program. The most secure and stable homes in America have parents who have a daily, radiant, lively, personal relationship with their Lord and Savior, Jesus Christ. Proverbs 14:26 tells us that the person who fears the Lord is like a secure fortress which serves as a refuge for their children.

The King David File: From a Nobody to a Champion

Today's world is in need of true heroes—people of integrity and strong character, whose lives inspire us. The Bible is packed with such men and women who faced some of the same culture crafters that we face in our lives. Already, we have seen how Daniel and his friends were prepared by King Josiah and their parents to live courageously in a pagan land. In this chapter, I want to show how God prepared a little ruddy, no-name shepherd boy to become a national champion and eventually the king of his nation.

If you are a parent, be assured that it is God's will for your children to be champions for God—spiritual giant killers. However, it's vital that we give God every opportunity to work His will, not *our will* for their lives. How can we do this? Start by praying daily that God will implant in your children the champion-like qualities mentioned below. Then let God put your children through His training program. God desires to direct their steps, even as children, and to carry out His plan for their lives.

Pray for Champion-Like Qualities

From the beginning, young David was no different from any of our kids. He had beautiful eyes, a healthy complexion, and was considered handsome. But he was nothing more than a young shepherd boy living outside Bethlehem when Samuel, the high priest, came looking for a king among Jesse's sons (see 1 Samuel 16:1-13). Jesse, the father of David, almost forgot to include David in the selection process: "Oh, yeah, there's still my youngest son, David. He's out back watching the sheep."

Samuel said to Jesse, "Send and fetch him."

The rest is history. The young nobody, whom even his father didn't consider to be "king material," became a champion for God. That's how God so often works.

I have noticed that when God looks for potential leaders on earth, He often looks for certain qualities. Genesis 6: 8, 9, tells us, "But Noah found grace in the eyes of the Lord. Noah was a just man and perfect in his generations, and Noah walked with God." And the Bible says of another man, "There was a man named Job, living in the land of Uz, who worshiped God and was faithful to him. He was a good man, careful not to do anything evil" (Job 1:1, *GNB*).

Is God looking for perfect people? No, but He is looking for people with the three champion-like qualities He found in David.

A Heart After God's Heart

"The Lord hath sought him a man after his own heart" we are told in 1 Samuel 13:14. What does it mean to be a person after God's own heart?

Charles Swindoll wrote, "Seems to me, it means that you are a person whose life is in harmony with the Lord. What is important to Him is important to you. What burdens Him burdens you. When He says, 'Go to the right,' you go to the right. When He says, 'Stop in your life,' you stop it. When He says, 'This is wrong and I want you to change,' you come to terms with it because you have a heart for God. That's bottom-line biblical Christianity."

God is still looking for such qualities today. The Bible says in 2 Chronicles 16:9, "God is always on the alert, constantly on the lookout for people who are totally committed to him" (*MSG*). The King James Version says it like this: "The eyes of the Lord run to and fro throughout the whole earth." Yes, even today God is searching for youth whose hearts are after His heart. Remember that God looks at the heart of your child, the innermost part of his or her spiritual being. God sees potential we don't see, and only God knows how to bring it to the surface.

At the age of seven, I confessed my sins and gave my life to Christ. To this day, I can remember the change of heart I experienced.

I remember feeling different, like my insides had been through a spiritual car wash. The change quickly made its way to the outside. I remember wanting to obey my parents, desiring to go to church, and telling my friends about Jesus. From that day forward, I had a heart after God's heart. Even though at times I struggled spiritually as a teenager, I knew that the most important thing in my life was to please God.

Dads and Moms, don't give up on your children! Pray for them. Pray with them. Have devotions with them. Talk to them about their relationship with Jesus Christ. Sacrificially give yourself to them for the cause of Christ. Let them see that Christ is the most important person in your life—not religion, not the church, but a vibrant relationship with Jesus Christ!

One day as I was listening to the radio, I heard Dr. Jack Hayford say something that I have never forgotten. He said that when his children were young, he took time to go away for days to pray and fast for them only. That made a deep impression on me. As busy as he was, pastoring a church of thousands, he took time out to fast and pray for his children. In May 2003, God let me see up close the fruits of Dr. Hayford's labor as I graduated from Trinity International's Divinity School with his son, Jack Hayford Jr. Certainly, God honored the prayers and fastings of Dr. Hayford, and He will honor ours as well.

A Servant's Heart

Why did God choose young David over his brothers to succeed Saul as king? The Psalms give us the answer: "Then he chose David, his servant, handpicked him from his work in the sheep pens" (Psalm 78:70, *MSG*). "I have found David my servant; with my holy oil have I anointed him" (Psalm 89:20).

Notice that while David was faithfully keeping his father's sheep, God called him "my servant." Even when David was a nobody working in the fields with animals known for their feeble-mindedness, God called him "my servant." God could have chosen a decorated soldier in Israel's army, or a young man in one of Israel's top schools, or even Jonathan, King Saul's son. Instead, He chose a quiet, humble young man who would continue to follow his father's orders, watching the sheep while his brothers were away fighting for their country.

One of my all-time favorite movies is *Hoosiers*. I grew up in Indiana, and like all true Hoosier kids, I ate, slept and drank basketball. One of my favorite scenes in *Hoosiers* is when Hickory High School is playing in the Indiana High School State Finals in Indianapolis. Hickory (the real name of the school was Milan) barely had enough boys to constitute a team, but won the state tournament, which originally started with over 300 high school teams. The father of one of the players, Shooter (actor Dennis Hopper), plays an alcoholic who is put in a hospital to dry out following a drinking binge. During the last minutes of the state finals, he nervously marches back and forth in his hospital robe, shouting, "I'm telling you, no small school has ever made it this far in Indiana high school basketball history."

Shooter was right. In over 100 years of Indiana high school basketball, Milan was the only small school to win the tournament. Stories like those told in *Hoosiers* don't happen very often in a humanistic world. But this real-life occurrence is a reminder to me of God's ways with His children—when God takes the least, the meager, the insignificant, and uses it to get the job done.

God hasn't changed. He still operates the same way. He looks for the lowly, the faithful, the humble servants. God cares about character, not a slick public persona. God knows the kind of people He wants, and He knows where to find them. It's my prayer that God's Spirit will slip into your home and will choose your child to be *His servant.*

A Childlike (Innocent) Heart

"So he [David] fed them [Israel] according to the integrity [completeness, innocence] of his heart; and guided them by the skillfulness of his hands" (Psalm 78:72).

A few years ago, pop music star Britney Spears recorded a song titled "Oops! I Did It Again." Shortly afterwards, I began to notice that young children and preteens were singing the last four words of the chorus, "I'm not that innocent," accompanied usually by a little swagger or attitude. Sadly, the idea of moral innocence even among children seems no longer popular. Pop culture today operates on the suspicion that if you look long enough and deep enough, everyone is hiding something—that no one can be morally pure.

But David was a man of integrity, morally pure and innocent. Yes, he was sharp-looking and impressive outwardly, but, more importantly, he understood the greater value of possessing a strong inner man. Obviously, this is why he penned Psalm 51:6: "Behold, thou desirest truth in the inward parts: and in the hidden part thou shalt make me to know wisdom." David too, would agree with Proverbs 20:27: "The spirit of man is the candle of the Lord, searching all the inward parts of the belly."

God is looking today for wholeness, completeness and innocence in the inward parts. He is looking for spiritual substance that God's Word calls the "righteousness of Christ." Will He find it in our homes and within our children? I believe He does and He will. However, the making of champions must start with moms and dads who are Christlike champions themselves.

God's Method of Training

Charles Swindoll writes about how God trained David: "His training ground was lonely, obscure, monotonous, and real." Let's briefly examine these four disciplines.

Solitude. God trained David in solitude. He spent much of his time alone with sheep under the stars. He endured mildly cold winters and long hot summers. He faced wolves, mountain lions and bears. David no doubt had a lot of time to think, meditate and talk with God.

The word *solitude* today has a negative connotation. Most youth might equate it with spending time in prison. As a society, we have surrounded ourselves with external sounds and sights. It's not cool to be alone . . . and definitely not cool to be surrounded by silence.

Clearly, David's youth was soaked both in solitude and silence. Nonetheless, these circumstances never warped his thinking. He never became a weirdo or a cult leader. The isolation didn't mar him socially. In fact, just the opposite was true. David became one of the greatest leaders in history.

John Maxwell wrote, "Your life today is a result of your thinking yesterday. Your life tomorrow will be determined by what you think today." Solomon wrote, "For as he thinketh in his heart, so is he" (Proverbs 23:7). In the soil of solitude David sowed good seed that reaped a harvest for a lifetime.

Obscurity. David grew up in obscurity. The value of obscurity is captured wonderfully by Chuck Swindoll: "God trains his best personnel in obscurity. Men and women of God, servant leaders in the making, are first unknown, unseen, unappreciated, and unapplauded. In the relentless demands of obscurity, character is built.

Over the last 25 years, an ever-increasing number of families have made the decision to home-school their children in America. According to the 2000 U.S. Census Bureau, 790,000 children from ages 6 to 17 were home-schooled in 1999, up from 360,000 in 1994. Those numbers represent more than a trend; they represent a national movement of colossal proportions. Why the radical home-school growth? We could point to a variety of factors, but I believe the underlying factor is the sovereign will of God. I see Almighty God raising up millions of children who have been taught in the obscurity of their homes by sacrificing parents who envision a champion for Christ in the future.

Monotony. Swindoll says monotony is just plain L-I-F-E, without the wine and the roses. It's being faithful in the menial, insignificant, routine, regular, unexciting, uneventful daily tasks of life. He refers to monotony as one of God's favorite methods of training—just constant, unchanging, endless hours of tired monotony as you learn to be a man and woman of God . . . with no one else around, when nobody else notices, when nobody else even cares.

David was not the only Biblical character who experienced years of monotony before being used greatly by God. Noah, Abraham, Joseph, Moses, Joshua, the disciples and the apostle Paul all received their degrees in monotonous education. Even our Lord spent 30 years of uneventful, daily monotony before beginning His public ministry that probably lasted no more than three and a half years.

In God's training program of champions, monotony seems to be the rule, with very few exceptions.

How do we as parents keep from getting in God's way of putting our children through His training programs? With X-Boxes, television, movies, sports, malls, music, church and school activities, youth today are constantly being entertained and stimulated. It's easy for parents to get caught up in the social web of activity and not give our heavenly Father space to work in our children's lives. As Christian families, we can become event-oriented, fitting God in when and where we can, hopeful that our children somehow will be forever spiritually impacted.

Life is not meant to be a roller-coaster ride, however. It is a journey, a process. I don't expect your teenager to agree, but *boring* can be a healthy thing. People have time to think, meditate, and even rest, when they are bored. Ordinary, dull, monotonous living slows us down so we can hear God's voice. I often tell the church I pastor that the most spiritual thing we can do sometimes is take a nap, get rest, and slow down our lives.

The following are some practical suggestions for giving God space in our lives to take us though His training program of monotony. Although these are not always convenient to implement, they are well worth the effort. Prayerfully consider how you might put them to work in your family.

1. Take several minivacations throughout the year in which you spend time with one another talking, praying, reading and discussing God's Word. Be sure to exclude television, radio and all other outside influences. Give yourselves to one another and to your heavenly Father.

2. Plan one or two nights a week in family activities without television and other outside influences. Let your evening include times of family prayer, devotions, games, watching family videos, going to a park, or visiting a shut-in or someone in a nursing home.

3. Encourage your children to keep prayer journals where they can write down what God is saying to them and doing in their lives. Encourage them to hear God speak and record His words to them as

they read God's Word. Attend worship services and Bible studies, and pray.

4. Show your children how to give of themselves to the poor, the needy and the hurting. Give them opportunities to be a part of urban ministry and to take mission trips.

5. Finally, don't clutter your child's life with activities. Spend time with them. Talk with them, play with them, cry and worship with them. Exalt Christ daily and He will draw your children unto Him.

Reality. What kind of man was David? He was a man of reality. He was real, responsible, and a man of integrity when nobody was looking.

Swindoll says that getting alone with God doesn't mean you sit in some closet and think about infinity. "No, it means you get alone and discover how to be more responsible and diligent in all the areas of your life, whether that means fighting lions or bears or simply following orders."

It is in our personal, secret place with God where the examining and judging of ourselves takes place. The word *judge* in the context of the Lord's Table in 1 Corinthians 11:31 means "to separate yourself." It is telling us to detach ourselves from everyone and everything, judging ourselves according to the Word of God. When we judge ourselves—confronting, confessing and repenting of personal sins, we can expect to be victorious in the public battles of life.

It was while David was monotonously tending his father's sheep in solitude and obscurity that a lion or a bear came and took a lamb from the flock. David went after the lamb and rescued it. When the animal attacked David, he seized it and killed it. David reminded Saul of this reality when Saul told David, "You can't fight this Philistine. You're just a kid" (see 1 Samuel 17:33). But David knew better. Even though he was young, he had been prepared in the secret place of the Almighty. He had confidence in his God. David saw himself as a champion who was up to any challenge.

The Only Stable and Secure Foundation

Isaiah 28:16, says, "Therefore thus saith the Lord God, Behold, I lay in Zion for a foundation a stone, a tried stone, a precious corner stone, a sure foundation: he that believeth shall not make haste." A person who acts hastily is an unstable person because his actions are not properly founded. This person is easily swayed and moved by the storms of trials and persecutions. We must constantly evaluate our foundation. What are we building our lives on? What is our foundation made of? Will it withstand the trials of the day—cancer, divorce, death of a loved one, severe disappointment, job loss?

As a pastor, one of the most difficult things about my job is watching people I shepherd and love go through painful and trying periods in their lives. At the same time, one of my greatest blessings comes from watching them come through these painful and trying periods victorious in their faith because their lives are built on Christ.

A young man I know is presently separated from his wife. Just a few weeks prior to the separation, he was converted, baptized in water and in the Holy Spirit. Now he lives every day in Christ Jesus. He is truly dying out to self, and the life of Christ is being lived in him. You would never know by being around him that he is going through such a difficult circumstance. He is living on a higher plane. His friends and family are incredulous that he has so much peace and joy, as well his as faith that God is in control. He is taking it one day at a time, believing God will restore his marriage. Only a life built on a sure foundation can bring that kind of stability and security.

Another example is Debbie, in her early 40s with four wonderful children. She has a beautiful home and marriage and is a gifted nurse. She and her husband are the kindest, most generous people one could ever hope to meet. He is a highly respected businessman and politician. They are known, loved and admired by hundreds of thousands of people throughout our tri-state area. But a few months ago, the doctors told Debbie her cancer is incurable. At the time of this writing, she has been fighting cancer for a nearly three years.

She has undergone treatments, surgeries, and all kinds of tests. She has been given one hopeless report after another by the medical experts, but you would never know it.

Debbie has the faith of a spiritual giant. Everywhere she goes, she testifies of God's wonderful grace and gives God the glory. She possesses the peace that comes only from God, which is greater than the cancer. She says that no matter whether she is healed on earth or in heaven, she will speak of God's goodness everywhere she goes. In the last few years, I have watched her lead people to Christ and share her faith in churches and gatherings of every kind. She is truly an example of a life built on Christ, the tried stone, a precious cornerstone, the only sure foundation.

Jesus once told his followers a story that lets us know we can build our house (our lives) either on the sand or on the rock. He said the foolish man builds on the sand, and his house collapses when the rains and the wind come. But the wise man builds his house on the rock, and his house will stand long after the rains and the wind have come and gone.

Is your foundation strong, secure and stable? Can it withstand the trials of life, the attacks of the Enemy, the deception of man? Be sure to build your life, your marriage, your family and your career upon the only sure foundation—Jesus Christ. He will not disappoint you.

DISCUSSION QUESTIONS

1. Can parents get in the way of God's training program for their children? How?

2. What can parents do to provide a climate in the home that can produce champions for Christ?

The Peer Crafters

Chapter Six

The following suicide notes were left by Japanese schoolchildren, ages 10 to 15, who chose to take their own lives within the last several years. Some of them met in suicide chat rooms, which are becoming increasingly popular in Japan (as well as in other countries). *Translated from Japanese by Patrick Luhan.*

Left by a 10-year-old boy who killed himself after being harassed for having an American father: " My blood is tainted and corrupt. I will fly from my apartment window, fall, and die. Why have I not died already? Because I have been waiting for tomorrow."

Left by a 14-year-old boy who hung himself: "I've always had my money taken from me. I could never have enough money to meet their demands, so they would hold me underwater until I agreed to do what they wanted. They'd always make me run errands for them. They forced me to dye my hair once. Getting bullied has become harder and harder, and I cannot go on with this life. Hopefully my death will excuse my failure."

Left in a notebook by a 15-year-old boy who threw himself from a high building: "T. hurts me all the time. I've avoided going to school. I hate his kicking and punching. I can't stand how often these things happen."

Left by a15-year-old boy who hung himself: "I am already tired."

Left by a 14-year-old boy who hung himself: "When I was in seventh grade, I was always bullied. Now in eighth grade, the bullying has become worse. They make fun of me, throw things at me, kick me, hit me, and do other violent things. It was a waste of time complaining to the teacher when I couldn't tolerate it. They'd throw my textbooks at me and harass me for telling the teacher. I have no friends who sympathize with me in class. My close friends in clubs outside school have learned to hate me, too. I'm too tired to hold out any longer. The world's not right for me."

One of three suicide notes left by a 14-year-old girl before she threw herself off a high building: "I've been bullied with words and violence almost every day, but no one's been nice enough to even notice my situation. I've been hurt every day with insulting words like "dirty" from all the boys in my class. They will finally get what they want and I will die. I can't take this life anymore. Mama and Papa, I'm really sorry, but I'm finished. I'm afraid of death, but I know this will be a lifelong torment. I'm very sorry. Goodbye forever."

Left by an 11-year-old girl who met an 11-year-old boy in a suicide chat room, they both hung themselves: "I think I might die now. I've prepared all the necessary tools. Bye-bye."

Peers have the capacity to influence each other for good or for bad. Sadly, sometimes the bad can be deadly. Peer pressure can be so strong that research shows that even when people know the correct answer they will choose the incorrect answer – just because everyone else is choosing the incorrect answer. These studies have also shown that all it takes for most people to stand their ground on what they believe is for one other person to join them. This principle holds true for persons of any age in various peer pressure situations.

Our peers influence us, whether we know it or not, just by the time we spend with them. It's human nature to listen to and learn from other people in one's own age group. Some kids give in to peer pressure because they want to be liked, some give in because they want to fit in. Others go along with the group because they don't want to be made fun of, while others may just want to try something new that everyone else is doing.

Be Like Everybody Else?

Parents face their own peer pressure. Parents often make children more vulnerable to peer pressure by conveying to their kids the importance of "fitting into" society's artificial standards. Dr. Kevin Leman, in a article "Dare to be Different," writes, "Unfortunately every generation seems to start a little earlier in the great quest to become just like everybody else. Every season brings a new "must have it" kid craze: Pokemon, Tickle-Me-Elmo, Nintendo 64, Barbie, Cabbage Patch, Beanie Babies, PlayStation 2."

So many parents start their child young with wanting them to look like and dress like everybody else, or have what everybody else has. But do we really understand the message we are sending to our kids? When we consider what "everybody else" is like, do we really want them to be like everybody else?

Dr. Leman points out that if your son is like "everybody else," his adult life may look like this: "He may marry and divorce within the first five years of his adult life. He may drift from partner to partner. If he marries or moves in with a woman who has already been divorced, he will merge his life with someone whom somebody else has already discarded.

If your daughter is like "everybody else," she may have a half-dozen sexual partners before she graduates college. Her sexual experience will actually make her less likely to have a successful marriage, leading to a number of broken relationships. All of this makes life pretty ugly and very complicated."

According to Dr. Leman, if you raise your children like "everybody else," they are going to turn out like "everybody else's" children. If I let my child watch whatever he wants on television, if I take up for him every time a teacher or coach disciplines him, if I let him pierce nose, tongue, or whatever he wants to pierce, if I drop him off at the cinema or at the mall to do whatever he wants, if I let him run around in a car when he turns 16 with whomever he wishes

– he's going to grow up to be like "everybody else." God help us not to be like everybody else!

When Support Systems Fail

There are many youth specialists today who play down the power of peer pressure. They say that what matters most to youth is pleasing their parents, not their peers. I don't doubt that, but what happens when parents are not actively involved in the lives of their children? What happens when parents are too busy or separated from their children due to divorce or work? What happens when youth become alienated from their parents because of substance abuse, sexual abuse, a change of sexual orientation, or crime? In other words, do youth still value pleasing parents over peers when their main social support system – the home is broken and dysfunctional?

For example, lets take a 16-year old boy who has no dad at home, whose mother works a full-time job and may even have a live-in boyfriend. Anymore, this is pretty typical. The boy becomes unusually peer dependent. If the peer group says that he needs to smoke dope to fit in, he'll smoke dope. If the peer group likes to drink on the weekend and then race their cars down a lonely highway, your peer-dependent son will follow along. If he finds a young woman who thinks he's fascinating, he'll spend all his time with her, and before long she's pregnant with his child.

A few years ago, CBN's (Christian Broadcasting Network) 700 Club did a great story on a good friend of mine. My friend, Tim, was born with webbed toes, webbed fingers, a cleft lip and pallet, and a speech impediment. Unfortunately, he was raised in a broken home where alcoholism played a prominent role. Because of Tim's physical appearance, he was often shunned and made fun of by his classmates while growing up. In his early teens, he turned to alcohol and then drugs. Tim was an alcoholic at the age of 15. Throughout his teen years, he continued to drink alcohol and do drugs to escape from a life of rejection and alienation. Thankfully, Tim at 21 years of age was invited to the church where I pastored in Terre Haute, Indiana. Tim wonderfully gave his life to Christ and was instantly delivered by the power of the Holy Spirit from the drugs and alcohol. A few years later, he met a young lady in our church who was a schoolteacher. Today, some 15 years later, they have a happy marriage and family. Both Tim and his wife, Michelle, teach school and serve as associate pastors in a growing church near Chicago.

Clearly, without a strong family support system, youth will more often then not turn to one another for support, acceptance, and sense of a self-worth. Obviously, 50 years ago, that was not the case. But because of the breakdown of the family and modern society's interlinking sense of community, today's youth spend more time than ever with their peers. What's scary is when teenagers number one source of acceptance and value comes from their peers. Why? Because inevitably there will be criticism, disapproval, and rejection. Then, when that support system fails, youth often become hopeless and may turn to drugs, alcohol, prostitution, the occult, or the most fatal of them all, suicide.

The New Forms of Families

In a Chicago Tribune editorial written by a college professor who co-chairs the Council on Contemporary Families, she concluded her article with these words: "My hope for the future is that we stop pretending family diversity will disappear and start figuring out how to help all of our families do a better job raising their children and sustaining their commitments."

Many share this woman's sentiment, that the supremacy of the traditional family will never again be the norm in America. She's right about family diversity today; we have social freedoms running out our ears! We have single-parent families, cohabitation families, male same-sex partners, female same-sex partners, multiple partner families, and the old-fashion types heterosexual marriages (remember them?). We now have the ability to have sex without getting pregnant and to get children without having sex. Are you confused yet? I liked it when it was simple - date while living at your parents, get married, have sex, and then have the baby. But according to the article's author, we are moving away from marriage and the traditional family. Therefore, she insists that we must find solutions for raising kids better and having longer sustaining commitments within the framework of these new forms of families.

The problem is that when these new forms of families and marriages are so dysfunctional, how can children have any kind of chance of survival, much less emotional and mental stability? How can a society promote strong, lasting relational commitments, when as a culture we endorse and encourage those activities that destroy and prevent permanent commitments? How can we successfully raise kids by teaching "There is no objective truth," or "Do what you think is best for you," or "Your personal freedom is all that matters."

What the author of this article has forgotten along with much of popular culture is this one solid, foundational truth from the Bible – it was Almighty God who ordained the ideal family unit to consist of a dad (husband), a mom (wife), followed by children. And when that unit functions according to the instructions handed down to us in the manual (the Bible), children are raised successfully and marriage commitments are sustained. Can there still be strong family support systems in place for today and tomorrow's youth? Absolutely, but doing things *by the book* (the Bible) must be the only way. The psalmist David understood this when he wrote in Psalms 1: 2 , 3, "But his delight is in the law of the Lord; and in his law doth he meditate day and night. And he shall be like a tree planted by the rivers of water, that bringeth forth his fruit in his season; his leaf also shall not wither; and whatsoever he doeth shall prosper."

"Bad Company"

The Apostle Paul inspired by the Holy Spirit wrote, "Do not be misled: 'Bad company corrupts good character " (1 Corinthians 15:33, *NIV*). I often convey to youth, you will attract what you are. The old saying is, "geese of a feather, flock together." If you don't want crows for friends, then don't look or sound like a crow and whatever you do, don't fly where crows fly. On the other hand, if you want to attract an eagle (which of course, don't flock), then you must act like one and soar where eagles soar. Certainly, you will have your times of lonesomeness, but you will eventually attract an eagle. It will be worth the wait and the perseverance.

The Book of Judges tells of a young man named Samson whom God had raised up to deliver Israel from "out of the hand of the Philistines" (Judges 13:5). God blessed Samson in his youth and the Spirit of the Lord began to move upon him on various occasions (vv. 24, 25). One time the Spirit of God came upon him and he killed 30 Philistines. On another occasion, the Spirit of the Lord came upon him and he wiped out a thousand Philistines with the jawbone of an animal. God used Samson greatly to deliver Israel from 40 years of Philistine oppression. Samson then judged Israel for 20 years.

Samson's rule and God's blessings could have lasted much longer had he not sought out some "bad company." Judges 16:1 says that he had sexual intercourse with a prostitute in Gaza. A few verses later, he began his legendary romance with Delilah. Delilah tried on three different occasions to get Samson to tell her what the source of his strength was. She was working with the Philistine FBI in a sting operation, hoping that Samson would divulge his secret. Apparently, the Philistines had decided that they could not physically match Samson, so why not bait him using his number one weakness—a beautiful woman.

Finally, Samson gave in, and it had nothing to do with her beauty. Actually, as Judges 16:16 explains, Delilah practically nagged him to death. He couldn't take it anymore. So Samson confessed... everything. She then called the Philistines in to bind him. She got her money. They got their man.

What do we learn from this story besides that nagging is like kryptonite? It can bring any super or not-so-super man to his knees. The real lesson learned is that Samson had everything going for him—the blessings and favor of God, success as Israel's judge, and victory over the Philistines; until he began to associate with bad company. Samson was like an eagle that begins to fly with the crows until eventually he is bound and caged. Fatefully, all eagles end up bound and caged when they associate with bad company. That's why the Bible warns us to not be misled by bad companions.

How to Attract "Good Company?"

Peers who possess the qualities of true friendship can influence us for good. Remember, we attract what we are. So if we want peers who will influence us for good, it's important that we possess the qualities that we are looking for in others. Proverbs 27:17 says friends influence one another for good, like iron sharpening iron.

The Bible gives us some important qualities to practice and possess if we are going to have healthy friendships. The most important quality is *unconditional love*. The first part of Proverbs 17:17 says "A friend loves at all times." You say, that's impossible! Only through a relationship with our Lord and Savior, Jesus Christ, can we truly love others unconditionally. As we love God with our whole heart, soul and mind, He gives us the capacity to love others. It's this kind of unconditional love that enables us to forgive the sins and flaws of others.

Another vital quality in healthy friendships is *truthfulness*. Many people in our culture think that being truthful with a friend is the quickest way to kill a friendship. But truthfulness accompanied by unconditional love will only strengthen a relationship, not weaken it. "Faithful are the wounds of a friend; but the kisses of an enemy are deceitful" says Proverbs 27:6.

The third quality of a healthy friendship is *dependability*. If we practice being dependable in word and in deed, we will attract peers who are also dependable. The apostle Paul called his friend Tychicus "a dependable servant" (Ephesians 6:21). A dependable person is someone you can always count on. A person who is like a fortress, a rock, someone who is strong and can hold up others. When we are "in Christ," He makes us a friend who is dependable.

Unconditional love, truthfulness, and dependability are just three of the excellent qualities that parents must teach their children to practice and to a look for in peers. Peers that influence our children and teens for good can be a great blessing to both, parents and children. *One sharpens the other.* As parents we should pray daily that God will send our children peers with the highest of godly standards and that our children will discern and desire godly characteristics in the peers they choose as their friends.

DISCUSSION QUESTIONS

1. Discuss the role that parents play in raising kids that are not afraid to be different. How can the courage to be different than "everybody else" be taught to children?

Countering the Peer Crafters: Creating a Family Support System

Chapter Seven

As stated in the previous chapter, a strong family support system is the number one line of defense against the power of peer pressure in our children's lives. But how does that happen? What are those things that must be cultivated in a child if he or she is going to stand against the crowd? And when do parents start the preparation?

Dr. Kevin Leman says that one of the best ways to fight percolating peer pressure is to create a sense of belonging and encouragement from the time your children are toddlers. "If you wait until adolescence to begin tackling this problem, you're going to make your life much more difficult. Your children need a place of refuge, acceptance and belief. They may experience more rejection during the years between 16 and 25 (relationships, school, job refusals) than they will for the rest of their lives."

Love and acceptance; the home as a place of refuge, encouragement and affirmation; a sense of self-worth—these are elements that grow strong family support structures. Creating this kind of climate in a home requires hard work, which is best orchestrated by parents full of the Holy Spirit. All these positive reinforcements, however, do not guarantee that the children will become disciples of Christ. There are still factors beyond a parent's control—primarily, a God-given free will. In the final analysis, children must choose for themselves to walk in obedience and desire a life-giving relationship with Jesus Christ. Nonetheless, most parents have at least 18 years to have their children with them in the greenhouse of home to nurture them to the best of their ability. Parents have the responsibility to do everything possible, with God's power assisting them, to make disciples whose lives will be forever producing fruit for Christ.

Creating a Climate of Love and Acceptance

Michael W. Smith, popular contemporary gospel songwriter and recording artist, often says that it was his parents' unconditional love that prevented him from going along with the crowd as a young man. Like many boys, Michael had his rebellious days, but he never fell so far that he couldn't find his way back. When his closest friends started living a partying lifestyle, Michael realized he was going to lose touch with them if he didn't follow along. But knowing he was loved and accepted at home helped him resist the temptation to go along with them. Here's how he describes it:

"In my case, my closest friends started going to all the parties. I knew there was nothing for me there, but my friends wanted me to be a part of that scene simply because they were. Deep inside I knew that if I didn't join them at the parties, there was going to be a change in our friendship, and there was. Monday-morning conversations were always about the weekend. I could literally feel my friends pulling away, because I couldn't talk with them about the parties. They were 'nice' to me, but the 'hang thing' was over. I didn't belong anymore. That was hard."

Later in the same book Michael explains one of the reasons he was able to stand against the crowd:

"My parents are definitely role models in my life. The main reason I was able to stand against the partying crowd was because I received the acceptance I needed at home. 'Fitting in' still mattered, but I didn't crave it like some others did. I knew my parents loved me, and I respected the way they lived their lives. They stuck with me through the hard times and demonstrated a consistent, unconditional love so that I never strayed so far that I lost my way."

Michael W. Smith underscores the point that if children receive unconditional love and acceptance at home, the less likely they will crave it from their peers. Youth want to know that their parents value them, that their parents genuinely love them, and that their love is not connected to their behavior or performance. Children need to be reminded that no matter what they do, their parents still love them. Of course, that's easier said then done. But if you are a disciple of Christ, His *agape* kind of love resides in you. You have the capacity to love them as described in 1 Corinthians 13:4-9 in *The Message*:

"Love never gives up. Love cares more for others than for self. Love doesn't want what it doesn't have. Love doesn't strut, doesn't have a swelled head, doesn't force itself on others, isn't always 'me first,' doesn't fly off the handle, doesn't keep score of the sins of others, doesn't revel when others grovel, takes pleasure in the flowering of truth, puts up with anything, trusts God always, always looks for the best, never looks back, but keeps going to the end. Love never dies."

My parents raised my brother, my sister and me with an *agape*, unconditional kind of love. Like all kids, we had our ups and downs. But none of us ever looked to our peers for love and acceptance. We had friends we occasionally did things with, but our lives revolved mostly around our family and our church family. We were raised in the '60s and '70s, before James Dobson and Focus on the Family, before all the family-friendly books and programs that we have today. Actually, my parents didn't seem exceptionally family-conscious—not in the same way many parents are today. During most of my school-age years, my mother attended nursing school and worked a second-shift job, while my father worked a first-shift job and took care of us in the evenings. Nevertheless, my parents set the climate in our home with the love of God. Because of God's *agape* kind of unconditional love in them, we were firmly planted and now bear the fruit of our godly upbringing in our marriages, our families, and our own relationships with Jesus Christ.

Home: A Place of Refuge

If the home or family is a place of refuge, children will be less likely to give in to peer pressure. What do we mean by a refuge? Proverbs 14:26 says, "In the fear of the Lord is strong confidence: and his children shall have a place of refuge." *The Message* renders it as, "The Fear of God builds up confidence, and makes a world safe for your children."

Not just any home can be a place of refuge. Only a home that fears, reverences, and is in awe of Almighty God and His commands are truly a place of refuge. Listen to the tone of the psalmist's words in Psalm 119:14-16:

" I have rejoiced in the way of thy testimonies, as much as in all riches. I will meditate in thy precepts, and have respect unto thy ways. I will delight myself in thy statutes: I will not forget thy word" *(MKJV)*. The psalmist was not speaking of a frightening kind of fear, but a kind of confidence and faith in God that results in rejoicing, respect and delighting oneself in God's Word.

Following are seven practical ways of making your home and family a place of refuge. I encourage you to implement these. As you do, you will see the Spirit of God make your home into a place where your children can rejoice in, meditate on, respect and delight in the Word of God.

Love. It all begins with Dad and Mom. *We must love God with all our heart, soul and mind.* Raise your love standard for God as high as you can. You can't fool your children anyway; they can measure better than anyone how much you love God. Let the love of God resonate throughout your home, so much so that your children and their friends will feel God's presence and love.

Think. Encourage and train your children *to choose to think on those things that are good, positive and uplifting.* Families should memorize and practice Philippians 4:8: "Finally, brethren, whatsoever things are true, whatsoever things are honest, whatsoever things are just, whatsoever things are pure, whatsoever things are lovely, whatsoever things are of good report; if there be any virtue, and if there be any praise, think on these things." Jesus gave a good reason for this principle when He said, "A good man out of the good treasure of his heart bringeth forth that which is good; and an evil man out of the evil treasure of his heart bringeth forth that which is evil: for of the abundance of the heart his mouth speaketh" (Luke 6:45).

Speak. Encourage and teach your children *to speak good, positive and uplifting words.* Ephesians 4:29 says, "Let no corrupt communication proceed out of your mouth, but that which is good to the use of edifying, that it may minister grace unto the hearers."

Worship. *Plan for times of family worship together.* Plan times of Scripture reading, singing, storytelling and praying together. These are times when you as a family boldly declare, "As for me and my house, we will serve the Lord" (Joshua 24:15). As the psalmist wrote, "Exalt ye the Lord our God, and worship at his footstool; for he is holy" (Psalm 99:5).

Discern. Promote and practice *discernment and sound judgment* as a family. With all the ungodly influences that come into our homes today, this is not optional. "But strong meat belongeth to them that are of full age, even those who by reason of use have their senses exercised to discern both good and evil" (Hebrews 5:14). God's Word is that strong meat that gives us the ability to discern between good and evil.

Give. Practice and promote *giving of yourselves and your things to the poor, the needy and the hurting.* Remember, as you do so, you are giving to Christ himself. Jesus said, "I was hungry and you fed me, thirsty and you gave me a drink; I was a stranger and you received me in your homes, naked and you clothed me; I was sick and you took care of me, in prison and you visited me.' The righteous will then answer him, 'When, Lord, did we ever see you hungry and feed you, or thirsty and give you a drink? When did we ever see you a stranger and welcome you in our homes, or naked and clothe you? When did we ever see you sick or in prison, and visit you?' The King will reply, 'I tell you, whenever you did this for one of the least important of these followers of mine, you did it for me!'" (Matthew 25:35-40, *GNB*).

If your family will practice sacrificial giving, your children will grow up to be givers instead of getters. They will truly learn "to be humble toward one another, always considering others better than yourselves" (Philippians 2:3, *GNB*). Focus less on self and more on helping others.

Play. *Families need to play together.* The home should be a place of laughter, joy, fun and happiness. The Bible says Jesus came to give us abundant life. All youth love to have fun and enjoy life. If your home is a happy place, your children will want to be there. They will bring their friends home too. Then, you as a family will have opportunities to influence your children's peers with the love of Christ and they will sense the presence of God in your home.

Inspiring Through Encouragement and Affirmation

I am second-generation Pentecostal. I was raised in the Church of God (Cleveland, Tennessee), and am licensed as an ordained bishop. I am blessed to have grown up in the church and to have served in churches that practice the gifts of the Spirit. One of the most beautiful times in a Pentecostal-Charismatic worship service is when the Holy Spirit speaks forth a prophetic word through a Spirit-filled believer for the body of Christ. Almost invariably, all in the congregation give their complete attention to what God is saying to the church. Paul wrote to the Corinthians, instructing them, "But the person who prophesies speaks to people for their upbuilding, encouragement, and comfort" (1 Corinthians 14:3, *ISV*). Paul was saying that a word of prophesy is God's way of encouraging the family of God; it always builds up, encourages, and comforts everyone who hears it.

The apostle Paul was an encourager. Everywhere he ministered, he encouraged people. In 1 Corinthians 14:29, he wrote, "Therefore, my brothers, desire the ability to prophesy"*(ISV)*. Acts 4:36 tells us that Paul was mentored by a man named Barnabas, whose name means "one who encourages."

As a pastor, I minister to people weekly who are weary, beaten down and discouraged. The Enemy has battled them all week, attempting to make them weak. As ministers, we can relate to Job 4:4:

97

"When someone stumbled, weak and tired, your words encouraged him to stand" (*GNB*). I like the way *The Message* translates it: "Your words have put stumbling people on their feet, put fresh hope in people about to collapse." Later in the book, Job himself reminds us that we encourage by more than just our words: "I smiled on them when they had lost confidence; my cheerful face encouraged them" (Job 29:24, *GNB*).

People need encouragement not only in the church but also at home. Actually, encouragement for God's people should begin in the family. The Bible says, in Ephesians 5:23, that God has made the man the leader of his home, and he is to cherish his wife and children. As he loves them with Christ's love, he will automatically encourage, affirm, build up and comfort his family. If the husband and/or father chooses to be passive instead of proactive, the entire family suffers and may look elsewhere for encouragement and affirmation.

One of the most obvious things to me as a pastor is the number of women and youth who receive little or no encouragement and affirmation at home. Most youth who do not get it at home seek attention from others in the way they dress, look or behave. Wives who don't receive encouragement and affirmation from their husbands may develop insecurities, along with low self-esteem. Both wives and children crave encouragement and affirmation from the leader of the home, the man. Confidence, strength and self-worth will radiate from family members when it is present. If it is absent, the consequences can be both painful and eternal for the family.

Unfortunately, a large number of families today do not have fathers who actively accept their leadership roles. Single moms who try to play the roles of both dad and mom to their children lead many of these families. I want to encourage single mothers to turn your lives over to Christ and look to Him for leadership in your home. He won't let you down. He will be that missing husband to you and the father your children need. If you think that sounds far-fetched, I would like to assure you I have seen Him fill those roles many times. The psalmist says of God: "A father of the fatherless, and a judge of the widows, is God in his holy habitation" (Psalm 68:5).

A Sense of Self-Worth

A home that provides love, encouragement and affirmation, as well as being a place of refuge, is still not complete without family members who have a sense of self-worth. The important question for parents is this: How do we instill self-worth in our children? No doubt, today's culture crafters think they have the answer. But the bottom line is, we have more and more youth who are taking their own lives, more youth who are turning to drugs and alcohol, and multitudes of kids who feel as if they have no hope and no future.

As a single or married parent, the most valuable contribution you can make to your child is to instill a genuine faith in Jesus Christ. James Dobson on his Focus on the Family Web site writes:

"What greater sense of self-worth could there be than knowing that the Creator of the universe is acquainted with me personally? That He values me more than the possessions of the entire world; that He understands my fears and my anxieties; that He reaches out to me in immeasurable love when no one else cares; that He actually gave His life for me; that He can turn my liabilities into assets and my emptiness into fullness; that a better life follows this one, where the present handicaps and inadequacies will all be eliminated—where earthly pain and suffering will be no more than a dim memory! What a beautiful philosophy with which to 'clothe' your tender child. What a fantastic message of hope and encouragement for the broken teenager who has been crushed by life's circumstances. This is true self-worth at its richest, dependent not on the whims of birth or social judgment or the cult of the superchild but on divine decree".

Can it really be that easy? With all the genetic and environmental factors that go into my child's makeup, shouldn't creating a sense of self-worth be more complex? Jesus said, "I am come that they might have life, and that they might have it more abundantly "(John 10:10b). God desires that your children possess a sense of self-worth, that your children live life to its fullest. God has made that possible by sending his Son, Jesus Christ, to pay the price for our sins and give us life through His resurrection. You can be assured that your children will possess a sense of self-worth as they develop an intimate relationship with their Creator.

DISCUSSION QUESTIONS

1. Discuss the author's seven practical ways of making your home a place of refuge. Rate your own home from 1 to 5 - poor being 1 and 5 being excellent.

                                    1   2   3   4   5

   Love for God
   Good Thinking
   Speaking, Affirming One Another
   Family Worship
   Discerning Between the Godly and Ungodly
   Giving of Yourselves
   Play Together as a Family

2. Discuss the importance of fathers consistently affirming and encouraging their children.

The Song Crafters

Chapter Eight

"And therefore, I said . . . musical training is a more potent instrument than any other, because rhythm and harmony find their way into the inward places of the soul, on which they mightily fasten, imparting grace, and making the soul of him who is rightly educated graceful."—Plato

Of all the crafters that shape and mold popular culture today, musicians may be the most influential of them all. Music is a pervasive force in modern culture. We hear it everywhere—in stores, elevators, cars, airports, restaurants, lobbies, and at sporting events. In fact, we hear it so much, we often don't notice its presence.

As already noted in chapter two, television uses music in movies, commercials, talk shows, sporting events, award ceremonies, and even in nightly newscasts. Television strategically uses music to arouse certain emotions in its viewers. Even now, when I hear the theme music from *Rocky*, I want to go out and run through the streets like Rocky did when he was training for the big fight. In the last few years, television commercials have been reverting to the music of the '70s to get the attention of people my age who were teens during that decade. Hearing certain songs can bring back old memories and stir up emotions that we experienced at a particular time in our lives.

The point is, we spend innumerable hours each day absorbing various kinds of music. Whether it's secular or Christian, music and the arts in general play a central role in shaping the values of society. Music often mirrors culture and can serve as a voice of the spirit of a culture. In this sense, artists can wield great influence within a culture by using their talents and gifts. Music often reveals societal themes and issues, and tells us a great deal about the culture itself. In today's modern pop culture, the vast majority of people are greatly influenced by various forms of art, especially music.

Music, Morals and MTV

For thousands of years, Western thinkers have freely admitted that art (and music in particular) plays a key role in shaping the morals of its culture. One of the first to recognize this was the ancient Greek philosopher Plato. In Plato's *Republic*, he had Socrates expel all poets (including most musicians) from his ideal city. Plato believed the primary aim of music was to attach feelings to deeds. He was convinced that in a well-ordered society, good deeds are rewarded by the emotions, which follow from moral approval. Music then, when used properly, serves to help connect the two and thereby reinforces the governing values of the community. When Plato decided to expel most musicians from the ideal city, he was simply recognizing the other side of the coin: that music can also be used improperly to attach wrong emotions to wrong actions and that in doing so it sets itself against the community as a rival source of moral value.

"I think all music is worship music because every song is amplifying the value of something," says Louie Giglio, founder of the Passion worship movement. "There's a trail of our time, our affection, our allegiance, our devotion, our money. That trail leads to a throne and whatever's on that throne is what we worship. And we're all doing a great job of it because God has created us to be worshipers. The problem is that a lot of us have really bad gods."

Plato never brought into question the lyrics of songs, but only how it influenced the listener's emotions and actions. Plato understood that this form of popular culture was in itself very commanding. He accentuated *how* it was said, more than *what* was said. In fact,

103

to judge from his *Republic,* the music of ancient Athens didn't even have lyrics. And it is here that we have the most to learn from Plato.

Plato believed that like musical lyrics, the characteristic sounds that make up a musical style also tell a story. These sounds are considered the morality of music—the performance, lyrics and style—the art form itself. David Orland in an article for *Boundless Webzine* explains, "Take, for example, punk rock. Even if you could remove all the singing from a punk album, a characteristic sound would still remain. And, in the case of punk, this characteristic sound is the sound of scorn and resentment. Similarly with rap music. Strip away the words from your typical rap album and what's left over is a pattern of rhythms that comes very close to the sound of crude physical threat (oddly, this often holds true even of rap songs that are supposed to be about love). Rock music also, by its very form, encourages a mentality that is subjective, emotional and sensitive. In all these cases, when you put the lyrics back in, the message does not change — it just becomes more literal and obvious."

Music then, is a powerful vehicle for moral meaning, especially for youth. Almost all youth have musical tastes and freely share those with their friends. Some youth proudly share their tastes with the entire community as they drive down the road with car speakers thundering. Nonetheless, musical preference in our culture is accompanied by an allegiance, a devotion to the community upon which it is founded and the values characterized by that particular community.

"When one adolescent asks another about his musical tastes, he is thus asking about much more than the contents of his CD collection," says David Orland. "He is in fact asking about the contents of his soul. And in a culture in which music has, with the sponsorship of the big recording labels, too often come to represent a perverted moral life, this soul is rarely innocent."

No one in pop culture today mixes images, lyrics and sounds more powerfully than MTV. When watching MTV, youth are lured with identification and various types of behavior that promote heterosexual and homosexual immorality, drug usage, alcoholism, rebellion, the occult, liberal political agendas and crime. Yet, in contrast to MTV, hundreds of Christian radio stations throughout America feature various kinds of popular Christian music along with Bible teaching programs. These kinds of lyrics and sounds encourage morality, faith, family responsibility, and loving God and others as we want to be loved by others. If Plato were alive today he would certainly advocate most Christian music along with other styles of music whose rhythm and harmony find their way into the inward places of the soul, imparting grace, hope and peace.

The Internal Power of Music

Dr. Richard G. Pellegrino, a medical doctor with a doctorate in neurology and neuroscience, knows a lot about the effect that music has on our emotions. He's been working with the brain for 25 years, and Dr. Pellegrino says that nothing he does can affect a person's state of mind the way one simple song can. Pellegrino has worked with opium overdose victims in a New York City emergency room. As overdosing patients struggled for breath, ER staff would work feverishly to prepare injections of Naloxone, a drug that binds the opium high.

So what does this have to do with music? Plenty. According to Pellegrino, listening to music generates chemicals called endorphins in our brains. These natural opioids produce a high that is chemically similar to a drug high. Experiments have shown that if you give Naloxone to a group of people and ask them to listen to their favorite music, it suddenly becomes an intellectual exercise, and the intensity of the emotions seems to diminish.

This makes sense. We've all experienced the emotions that accompany music. That's why we listen. The promise of emotional impact is why you're more likely to hear the theme from *Rocky* than a Celine Dion ballad at a sporting event. The people in the sound booth want to create a mood, and they know that music is a powerful way to do it.

But getting this effect while dumping verbal garbage into your brain is much like getting high on opium. It may feel so great that you don't want it to quit, but ultimately, you're doing great damage to yourself. As Dr. Pellegrino told me, "You can pour messages in, and if you pour the *wrong* messages in, they take on a particular *power* more than the listener understands."

The Downward Spiral

Certainly, over the last 40 years, a moral erosion has taken place in pop culture's music. A bit of music trivia demonstrates the extent of the fall in pop music's romantic relationships:

1964 – The Beatles sing, "I Want to Hold Your Hand."

1967 – The Rolling Stones make a bolder overture with "Let's Spend the Night Together."

1972 – The Raspberries encourage the object of their affection to "Go All the Way."

1978 – Meatloaf describes in detail his version of "Paradise by the Dashboard Light."

1981 – Olivia Newton-John beckons a lover to get "Physical."

1987 – Inhibitions and euphemisms disappear with George Michael's brazen declaration, "I Want Your Sex."

1991 – Color Me Badd crudely and unflinchingly declares, "I Wanna Sex You Up."

1994 – Exactly 30 years after The Beatles first proposed hand-holding, R&B artist R. Kelly scores a best-selling single with sexually descriptive ode to intercourse, "Bump & Grind."

1997 – Janet Jackson describes sexual encounters with "Go Deep."

2002 – Eminem in "Love Me" uses his Shock & Awe style with lyrics filled with profanity, violence and sexual perversion. Romantic music has reached an all-time low.

Clearly, since the British Invasion of the '60s, popular music has been sliding into the sewer. Consequently, it has taken the culture with it. Whether they admit it or not, when musicians mix images, lyrics and sounds, they powerfully influence people's minds and emotions, especially young people's. Music plants thoughts and ideas, incites emotion, and carries with it (as we have already discussed) characteristic sounds. Unquestionably, there are some musicians who take their cues from life itself; and then, there are musicians who get great satisfaction when pop culture takes its cues from their music.

One of these is the widely popular rap artist Eminem. He raps, "So many lives I touch, so much anger aimed in no particular direction just sprays and sprays, and straight through your radio waves it plays and plays, till it stays stuck in your head for days and days."

Artists like Eminen claim they are just striking a chord with people, that they can't help it because so many people identify with their music and message. They claim they are not doing anything wrong, just exercising their free speech, when in reality, musicians like Eminem and many other rapsters are creating a culture of violence that is increasingly enveloping our children, desensitizing them to consequences and ultimately cheapening the value of human life. In the world of gangsta rap music, a segment of its music makes killing and the gangster life look cool. This music, reinforced by television through MTV and other music channels has spawned its own subculture, setting standards for how to dress, how to treat women, and how to resolve conflict through violence. When music in general preaches hate, violence and perversion, it only empowers fans to practice the same, to rebel and throw off the constraints of a lawful society.

To cite just a few reprehensible examples, consider a song like "Slap a Hoe" by the group Dove Shack, which touts the virtues of a machine that automatically smacks a wife or girlfriend into line, or the vile work of the death metal band Cannibal Corpse, which recorded one song describing the rape of a woman with a knife and another describing the act of masturbating with a dead woman's head.

On September 7, 1994, Officer William Robertson and his partner were responding to a call for police assistance when tragedy struck. As they pulled their van into a Milwaukee neighborhood looking for an alleged disturbance, one of the two teens who had placed the call signaled the other from a telephone booth. The trap was sprung. Using a high-powered rifle, a young sniper fixed the crosshairs of his telescopic sight on his prey, then fired. Robertson slumped dead in his seat. After an intense investigation, homicide detectives found that the murderers hadn't targeted Robertson specifically. The bored teens, who claimed to be taking cues from rapper Tupac Shakur's album, *2Pacalypse Now*, simply wanted to kill a police officer for amusement.

As a part of a 1997 Governmental Affairs Committee report, Senator Joseph Lieberman issued the following statement: "We are just learning, though, what appears to be a very real criminal connection within elements of the rap industry—links to racketeering, money laundering, gang violence and drug running. Death Row Records, which gave us Tupac and Snoop Doggy Dogg and which was in business with Time Warner and then Seagram, is now the subject of an extensive Federal investigation involving the FBI, the DEA and the IRS. Among other things, these authorities are examining Death Row's ties to one of Los Angeles' most notorious crack dealers who is now serving a 28-year prison term and who claims he provided more than $1 million, likely the proceeds of drug sales, in seed money to launch Death Row."

No End in Sight

Has the spiral reached bottom yet? Unfortunately, it will get much worse. How do I know that? Because today's children are bitter, angry and hurting, and they are crying out for attention. Unless we solve the crisis in our homes, we can expect more offshoots of dysfunctional and broken homes to parade and promote their degenerate lifestyles through music.

This morning, I read a *USA Today* editorial column titled "Our View: Broken marriages, not gay nuptials, pose risk to kids." The editorial in a nutshell was saying to the heterosexual community, how can you condemn same-sex marriages on the basis of saying gay marriages hurt children when studies on families point to a far more common reason that children increasingly are put at risk: the breakup of heterosexual marriages. The article went on to cite research that concludes that children growing up in single-parent homes suffer education failures, lawlessness, drug use and suicide at rates two to three times those of children raised by married parents. From there, the article gave more statistical evidence showing how single-parent or divorced-parent homes hurt children.

The editorial goes on to say, "Considerable evidence does document that children face fewer problems when married mothers and fathers bring them up. But even the most ardent opponents of gay marriage concede their claims that gay unions will hurt children are based on supposition and anecdotal evidence. Scientific studies about the impact of gay unions on traditional families are lacking."

The author of the editorial concedes that children who are raised by mothers and fathers who are married to each other do face fewer problems than single-parent or divorced-parent families. Not so surprising, is it? Also it advocates that we not condemn same-sex marriages until enough evidence comes in to show how gay marriages impact children. What they are basically saying is that the numbers haven't come in yet to prove that gay marriages hurt or help children.

What the editorial does not address is how same-sex couples often contribute to the single-parent family statistics before they choose to live together. What do I mean? Often, many homosexuals leave a heterosexual marriage or a live-in partnership, leaving children that they have raised or are still raising. Also, we should consider that there are many bisexuals in the gay community who have children, and many of these are single parents.

Additionally, there are gay couples who have adopted children or who may have children from a surrogate dad or mother who are still considered single or divorced parents due to state laws keeping them from marrying legally. Realistically, you cannot separate same-sex couples from single parents or divorced parents, because homosexuals often contribute to the single-parent/divorced-parent statistics.

We do have evidence, however, that indicates to us how same-sex marriages would impact children. As stated in chapter four, a Dutch study shows that the average homosexual relationship lasts only one and a half years and that gays in so-called committed relationships have an average of eight partners a year. One dirty secret that the media tries to hide is that research consistently finds gay relationships to be transitory and promiscuous in nature.

So I ask you, given this kind of environment, how can gay couples raise normal, well-adjusted, emotionally and morally stable kids? How can we expect children living with gay parents to work through all the confusion, complexities and the harassment they will deal with from society as a whole? Statistics do show that the farther you get away from children being raised by a mom and dad who are married, the higher the probability that kids will do drugs, drink alcohol, commit crimes, be sexually promiscuous, and be victims of divorce themselves someday. Children being raised by two moms or two dads, or one mom acting like a dad, or a dad acting like a mom is about as far as you can go from traditional marriage. This is why Romans 1:26-28 calls homosexual relationships "unnatural" and "inconvenient."

Am I picking on the gay community? No, because some heterosexual marriages and single-parent homes produce bitter, angry and hate-filled children as well. But if we as a culture keep diluting the institution of the family as God set in order, which is a husband, wife and children, we are going to see many more Eminems, Snoop Doggy Doggs, Michael Jacksons and Marilyn Mansons promoting unimaginable things even worse than murder, suicide, rape, drugs and sexual immorality. You say, "It can't get any worse"? We said that in the '70s concerning the sexual revolution. If history teaches us anything, we must see there is no end to how deceived and wicked a civilization can become.

Learning While They're Listening

According to a committee of the American Medical Association (AMA), "The average teenager listens to 10,500 hours of rock music between the seventh and 12th grades." What's more, the AMA reports, "As adolescents gain independence, they turn to music as an information source about sexuality and alternative lifestyles, subjects that are largely taboo." In other words, many youth today are turning to song artists to educate them or *to fill them in* on topics that are not a part of the public discourse.

Probably even more disturbing for people of faith is how deeply this music influences teens who attend church. Pollster George Barna discovered that, on a percentage basis, more Christian teens watch MTV each week (42 percent) than non-Christians (33 percent). "Our research," explains Alan Weed, president of the Christian music organization Interlinc, "indicates that Christian kids listen to four hours of music a day—most of it mainstream, not Christian."

What do these statistics mean to us who are Christians? First of all, we see that many Christian parents have failed in teaching discernment and sound judgment to their children regarding listening to music. Also, it is another indication of how even Christian parents don't have a clue to what kinds of music their kids are listening to.

As I mentioned earlier, my wife and I are the proud parents of a preteen son. We are in the process of teaching him discernment and sound judgment regarding television, movies and music. Admittedly, we too are receiving an education as we go down this path. Since his days of lying in a baby crib, he has listened to Christian contemporary music. At different times, he has been exposed to different kinds of secular music: rock, rap, classical, country and jazz. As a family, we have always tried to take time to talk about the music we hear: the lyrics, the sounds, the beat and the artist. We talk about what God expects of us as followers of Christ, and we define Biblical standards that will help us to determine what kinds of music we should listen to.

Recently, our son received a rap Christian CD from another believer. My wife and I listened to a couple songs on the CD, noting there were references made by the artist to his selling of crack on the streets before he was saved. After we discussed it as a family, we decided that it was something we would rather not have in our home. Even though the lyrics were Christian, the music copied the mainstream culture style of gangsta rap. We decided that if we permitted our son to listen to this particular rap CD, as well as others like it, we could be making it easy for him to develop a listening habit toward that particular style of music, whether it contained Christian or non-Christian lyrics.

I realize our decision could be argued against and debated. But my point is this: As parents, we have the responsibility to prayerfully discern all aspects of the music our kids listen to and then discuss it as a family according to the Biblical standards given to us by God. Too many parents refuse to let their kids listen to certain kinds of music without addressing the *why* questions. These questions are excellent opportunities to model and teach kids discernment and how to make wise choices in their lives. If we take the time to teach discernment, there will be less rebellion and defiance in our homes. Proverbs 2:11 reminds us, "Discretion shall preserve thee, understanding shall keep thee."

I learned about the potent power of music fairly early in my life. Throughout most of my childhood and early teens, I was blessed to have a best friend whom I will call Bob. Bob and I were tight, so tight we were inseparable. We were together mainly at church, and we would often spend the night at each other's home. We played a lot of sports together, especially basketball. We prided ourselves that no one could beat us at a game of two-on-two, or two-on-three for that matter. It was as if we could read each other's mind, especially on the basketball court. We were knitted together for life, or so it seemed.

But all that began to change when we were both about 13. It happened slowly, over a three-year period. Something began to come between our close-knit relationship, and it wasn't girls. Amazingly, it was music. Bob began to listen to certain rock bands that I just had no interest in. He became a KISS band fanatic. He had all their albums. At times he would dress up like Gene Simmons, and his school friends began to associate him with KISS.

I started to notice that instead of playing sports or just hanging out at his house, he wanted to listen to rock albums constantly. Soon, he began spending time with other school friends who also liked KISS and other rock bands as much as he did. He was spending money on albums recklessly and going to concerts. He and I were growing farther and farther apart. Even now, I recall the pain I felt on losing my best friend, not to someone else, but to the controlling influence of rock music.

Bob went on to attend a secular college and I attended a Christian college. From time to time, I would hear from mutual friends of Bob's continuous partying and living a wild lifestyle. Now, some 30 years later, I pray for Bob. I still cherish the great childhood we spent together and the precious memories we shared. But at the same time, I often wonder how things might have been different if it wasn't for the powerful influence that rock music had on his life. Undoubtedly, it was the music that introduced Bob to the world of alcohol and drugs, and it was the music that the Enemy used to plant seeds of rebellion early in his teen years.

How far can music influence a life? The answer is, as far as the listener will allow it. If a person, especially a young, impressionable teen, listens to the same song or CD over and over, day after day, he can't help but be influenced by its message: "For as he thinketh in his heart, so is he" (Proverbs 23:7). But then there is a supernatural, demonic influence that must be considered as well. Many rock artists openly admit to having occult and witchcraft beliefs, and many give themselves over to demonic influences through drugs and sexual perversion. Can this kind of evil, demonic influence be transmitted through music? Of course, it can. On the other hand, we can also ask, "Can the Spirit of God influence a person through music?" We know the answer to that. Christian songwriters, musicians and performers have had a wonderful influence for good on many.

The Bible reminds us in John 10:10a: "The thief [Satan] cometh not, but for to steal, and to kill, and to destroy." And he uses some song crafters as his messengers to plant, water and nurture seeds of destruction.

Can Satan's strategy be spoiled? Can he be exposed? Can the powerful influence of music be countered? How do we prevent people, especially youth, from being deceived by Satan's song crafters?

DISCUSSION QUESTIONS

1. If music can serve as a voice of the spirit of a culture, can it also serve as the voice of the spirit of an individual? What does today's music of choice among youth say about the spirit of today's youth culture?

2. Discuss how pop music over the last 40 years as influenced our culture? Does pop music mirror the culture or does the culture take it cues from pop music?

Countering the Song Crafters: *Developing Discernment*

Chapter Nine

The old saying "Catch a fish and you feed a man for a day. Teach a man to fish and you feed him for lifetime" can also be applied very well to parenting. Parents cannot keep watch over their children every minute for a lifetime, but parents *can* equip their children with tools to make wise choices regarding music. Sadly, most families struggle in their efforts to determine the right guidelines for listening to music. Some parents say no to virtually everything. Others search for a happy medium but still become frustrated, not knowing where to draw the line. Often their kids are equally confused. What, then, is a workable approach that allows the freedom to be "entertained" without harmful side effects?

Bob Waliszewski, in Focus on the Family's Webzine, writes, "The young people who most successfully navigate the land mines of today's entertainment are the ones whose parents take an active part in teaching and modeling wise choices. Just as you taught your child elementary skills like tying his shoes and riding a bike, you can ingrain in him the tendency to ask this question whenever considering a movie, video or musical selection: Would Jesus watch or listen to this? No matter what the child's age, it's not too late to introduce this question and encourage discernment."

More than ever, Biblically-based safeguards need to be employed to help today's youth be free of the destructive and ungodly messages of today's culture. But let me add, it is essential that Dad and Mom practice what they preach. If something is off limits for our children, why should it be OK for us as parents to listen to or watch? Shouldn't Biblical standards apply to everyone in our families, not just the children? Parents have what seems to be at times an impossible task, but God will honor any parent who takes the time to teach Biblical discernment regarding entertainment choices.

Questions That Provoke Discernment

The following questions may be used to crack open the door of discernment for youth. I suggest that you be careful not to use these questions to interrogate or agitate. They should be used with wisdom and patience with the goal of encouraging teens to practice discernment in regards to music.

- *What is it about this form of music that attracts you? Why do you like this particular style more than others?*
- *How does this form of music make you feel?*
- *Do the themes reflect reality? Do they reflect truth? If they reflect reality, do they also gloss over evil?*
- *How do the messages conveyed compare with the values you've been taught here at home or in church?*
- *Would you feel comfortable if Jesus sat here listening to or watching this with you? (See Matthew 28:20.)*
- *What do you think He'd say about this particular entertainment title?*
- *Does this entertainment have an opinion of God? What is it?*
- *What would happen if you imitated the lifestyles and choices of the characters in these songs or this program?*
- *Is there inappropriate entertainment? Where would you draw the line? Where does Scripture draw the line? Are they the same?*
- *How does it make you feel to know that by purchasing a CD you are supporting the morals and ideas that it's promoting?*

• *What subtle messages being conveyed through this entertainment? Do you agree or disagree with them?*

The Dumbing Down of Christians

I have served as a pastor for nearly 24 years. During that time, I have had the privilege of serving and ministering to countless numbers of families, and I have never heard a parent express a desire to teach discernment or establish family standards on the topic of entertainment. For the majority of even Christian families, we seem to have very little appetite for discernment regarding entertainment. It's as if many Christians are too proud to admit that standards are needed for what we watch and listen to in our homes.

To illustrate this, most of us remember what made the 2004 Super Bowl more memorable than previous ones. It wasn't the great game played between the New England Patriots and the Carolina Cougars. It wasn't the game-winning field goal. It wasn't even the million-dollar commercials. Unfortunately, everyone knows it was the exposure of Janet Jackson's breast.

The Monday morning following the Super Bowl, I was driving my son to school when I heard our local Christian disc jockey go on a rampage about the halftime show the night before. He mentioned that he and his small children were sitting enjoying the show until Justin Timberlake engineered, in Timberlake's own words, "a wardrobe malfunction." The radio DJ expressed how shocked and embarrassed he was for his children when they saw what had happened. He ended his segment by saying he and his family would not be watching any more halftime shows until the NFL cleaned up its act.

This radio personality was like millions of others who were insulted by what seemed to be an intentional attempt on Janet and Justin's part to shock the world. Many of these watching families called CBS, the FCC and their local congressman to express their disapproval. The NFL, CBS and Miss Jackson, along with Mr. Timberlake, all issued apologies. Several networks made a few cosmetic viewing changes. The FCC was called in for a congressional hearing. Nonetheless, three months later (at the time of this writing), nothing has really changed in the television world. Everything is pretty much back to normal until the next big shocking event occurs. We seem to be like the proverbial frog in the frying pan that is slowly being cooked, and every once in a while we complain when the heat is turned up a little too much for our comfort.

My question is "Why did it take an exposure of a breast to wake up everyone to the sleaze bath that viewers were enduring long before Janet and Justin's "shock and awe" bomb? Didn't the series of sexually suggestive dance moves while Timberlake sang "I'll get you naked before the end of this song" kind of serve as a warning to parents that it was time for a family raid of the refrigerator? And what about the raunchy, bump-and-grind sex show, featuring P. Diddy, Nelly and Kid Rock, before Jackson and Timberlake?

Just in case you are not a Super Bowl halftime junky, Sean "P. Diddy" Combs is not exactly "Up With People." Matter of fact, his version of "Up With People" would probably take on a whole new meaning. To give you a clue of what his life and music is all about, his record label is Bad Boy Entertainment. In 1999, he was ordered into anger management counseling for an assault on a record executive. In 2001, he was cleared of attempted murder, assault and bribery charges stemming from a New York nightclub shooting. One look at the lyrics of P. Diddy, Nelly and Kid Rock and you will wonder if the NFL in the NFL Halftime Show doesn't stand for *National F-bomb League*.

Wake up! The majority of Christians in America today seem to be "dumbing down" and going the way of the culture as a whole. What happened on stage in Houston on Super Bowl Sunday should come as no surprise to anyone who has watched even a few minutes of the crude programming that can be viewed daily on MTV. And even if you are smart enough not to go near MTV, cable television along with prime-time networks are overflowing with this kind of sexual titillation and exploitation. Pete Winn, the associate editor for *Family News in Focus*, wrote, "The real issue wasn't that Janet Jackson's breast was exposed. The real issue is that it exposed the fact that the Emperor has been wearing no clothes at all—and we've been going along with it."

Developing Discernment

Be Controlled by the Spirit. The Bible tells us there is a war that rages inside all of us, a war between human flesh and God's Spirit. The war is real, and the stakes are high. Romans 8:5, 6 says, "Those who live as their human nature tells them to, have their minds controlled by what human nature wants. Those who live as the Spirit tells them to, have their minds controlled by what the Spirit wants. To be controlled by human nature results in death; to be controlled by the Spirit results in life and peace" (*GNB*).

The apostle Paul says in Galatians 5:16, 17, "What I say is this: let the Spirit direct your lives, and you will not satisfy the desires of the human nature. For what our human nature wants is opposed to what the Spirit wants, and what the Spirit wants is opposed to what our human nature wants. These two are enemies, and this means that you cannot do what you want to do" *(GNB).*

The first key to discernment is to be led or controlled by the Spirit of God. God puts His Spirit in all of us when we are converted to Christ. As we yield ourselves to His Spirit, good things will happen inside of us. Galatians 5:22 says, "The Spirit produces love, joy, peace, patience, kindness, goodness, faithfulness, humility, and self-control" (*GNB*).

On the other hand, Galatians 5:19-21 says that if we our controlled by our flesh, "it shows itself in immoral, filthy, and indecent actions; in worship of idols and witchcraft. People become enemies and they fight; they become jealous, angry, and ambitious. They separate into parties and groups; they are envious, get drunk, have orgies, and do other things like these" (*GNB*).

The God of the Bible commands His people in Ephesians 5:18, "Be filled with the Spirit." He says instead of being drunk with wine and controlled by its influence, drink of the Holy Spirit and be controlled by Him. The apostle Paul, under the inspiration of the Holy Spirit, in the next few verses tells us that being filled with the Spirit will give us the ability to discern the kind of music we are to listen to and sing. *The Message* translates verses 19 and 20 like this: "Sing hymns instead of 'drinking' songs! Sing songs from your heart to Christ. Sing praises over everything, any excuse for a song to God the Father in the name of our Master, Jesus Christ."

God is saying to us, "Be filled with the Spirit and I will put a song in your heart." And when God puts a song in your heart, you don't have to worry about exercising discernment in your music anymore! His songs will be from your heart to Christ. They will be songs filled with praise to God in Christ Jesus.

Does this really work? Can we be so filled with the Holy Spirit that He puts His songs in us?

One of the joys of being a pastor is watching people grow in Christ and be filled with His Spirit. Suddenly, they don't prefer listening to Willy and Waylon anymore, or the Judds, or Billy Joel, or the Rolling Stones, or Snoop Doggy Dogg. God's Spirit takes the taste for the world's music off their hearts' hard drives and puts His song in them. Sure, they may choose contemporary Christian over Southern gospel, or their preference might be praise and worship music. But inherently, people who are controlled by and filled with the Spirit of God want to listen to music that will edify and build them up. As we drink of the Spirit of God, He keeps filling us and all we want is more of Him. There is no room or desire for the world's music or message anymore.

Know the Truth. When the Holy Spirit controls us, John 16:13 says, He will reveal the truth about God and He will lead us into all the truth. The truth is what enables us to discern between good and evil. It is the truth (the Word of God) that we must hide in our hearts, so we will not sin against God (Psalm 119:11). Listed below are various truth principles from God's Word. The Holy Spirit uses these truths to help us to discern between what is right and what is wrong. The key is to know and obey the truth, and it will set us free from sin and its hold on our lives.

Scripture Locations	**Discernment**
Exodus 20:1-17	The Ten Commandments helps us to know and understand the basic moral law of society.

Deuteronomy 18:10, 11	Warns us to stay away from occult practices such as divination, sorcery, fortune-telling, witchery, casting spells, holding séances, or "channeling" with the dead
Psalm 1	Warns us to beware of ungodly counsel, ungodly associations, and those who criticize and scorn others
Psalm 101	David's pledge of purity to the Lord
The Proverbs	Teaches valuable truths in the areas of finances, sexual temptations, family responsibility, work ethics, wickedness, gossip, righteousness, and basic lessons on human depravity
Malachi 3:9-12	Instructions in the area of financial prosperity—the blessing and the curse
Matthew 5:1-10	Instructions on how to live the blessed life
Matthew 6:21-24	Protecting the eyes
Matthew 13:4-23	Instructions on the four conditions of the heart that hear the gospel preached
Matthew 24	Signs Jesus gave concerning how we would know when the end of the world is near
Romans 12:1-2	Don't be conformed; be transformed.
1 Corinthians 13	Instruction in how to practice the love of God
Philippians 4:4-8	Your heart's best defense!
1 Thessalonians 5:21	Test everything!
1 Thessalonians 4:3-8	Control your passions.

| 1 Timothy 4:7-16 | Instructions for young Christians |
| 2 Timothy 4:3, 4 | Don't waffle on the truth. |

Build a Strong Defense. One of the ways I give myself a break from pastoring is by coaching basketball. The first year I coached, my kids couldn't pass the basketball very well. They were fourth- and fifth-graders who were just learning the fundamentals of the game. Since we couldn't pass the ball, that meant we couldn't run any kind of offensive plays. So we decided the one thing we could do is work at playing great half-court, double-teaming defense. We figured if we could get lots of steals, all we had to do was dribble the ball down the court and make layups.

That year, we had begun the season by losing our first five out of six games. But after we implemented our half-court defense, we started stealing the basketball on almost every play and dribbling down the court and making layups. It worked! One team that beat us by 30 points in the second game of the year, we beat at the end of the year. Our team won the last six games. Why? A great defense makes a good offense!

I love Ephesians 6:10-18; it is the armor of God we must put on daily. First, when I pray, I put on the belt of truth. The truth holds everything together. I then put on the breastplate of righteousness, which covers the heart, my emotions and passions. Next, I put on the shoes that prepare me to stand firm and profess the good news of the gospel. Then I carry the shield of faith, so that I may block and extinguish the fiery temptations of the Enemy. From there, I put on the helmet of salvation, which guards my mind from impure thoughts. Finally, I put on the sword of the Spirit, which is the Word of God that serves as my offensive weapon. It is God's Word that defeats the Enemy.

In Ephesians 6:11-14, we are told to put on the armor of God, and four times we are told to stand against and withstand the schemes of the devil. The idea is that we can stand with God's armor on and the Enemy's tactics will actually break on us. The picture here is similar to an image that Winston Churchill once used to describe a favorite British general; Churchill said, "He was like a frozen peg driven into the ground." When we as Christians stand with God's armor on, we are an immovable force that frustrates the Enemy.

Go on the Offensive! Standing with the armor of God on is not enough. We must go forth into Satan's territory, tearing down his kingdom and building the kingdom of God. God has called His church to be a church on the offensive!

What does this have to do with developing discernment? Everything. If you are on the defensive all the time without employing the spiritual offensive weapons God has given you, your discernment will wear down after a while. Most football fans know that if the offense doesn't move the ball, the team's defense sooner or later will become tired and start giving up points. Many Christians today defend or guard their faith, but very few are moving the gospel forward into the Enemy's territory.

God's playbook gives some great offensive plays. I love 2 Corinthians 10:4, 5: "The weapons we use in our fight are not the world's weapons but God's powerful weapons, which we use to destroy strongholds. We destroy false arguments; we pull down every proud obstacle that is raised against the knowledge of God; we take every thought captive and make it obey Christ" (*GNB*). *The Message* makes it sound a little more vicious: "We use our powerful God-tools for smashing warped philosophies, tearing down barriers erected against the truth of God, fitting every loose thought and emotion and impulse into the structure of life shaped by Christ. Our tools are ready at hand for clearing the ground of every obstruction and building lives of obedience into maturity."

What are these mighty weapons that God has given us?

The Sword of the Spirit, God's Word. Psalm 119:9-16 says, "How can young people keep their lives pure? By obeying your commands. With all my heart I try to serve you; keep me from disobeying your commandments. I keep your law in my heart, so that I will not sin against you. I praise you, O Lord; teach me your ways. I will repeat aloud all the laws you have given. I delight in following your commands more than in having great wealth. I study your instructions; I examine your teachings. I take pleasure in your laws; your commands I will not forget" (*GNB*).

Praying Always—Ephesians 6:18. If the Bible teaches us anything about prayer, it is that persevering, travailing, agonizing prayer is the Christian's *shock and awe* air campaign that demolishes the strongholds of the Enemy. Satan has no answer for persevering prayer.

Throughout my ministry, I have seen prayer bring down major satanic strongholds. One time during my pastorate in Terre Haute, Indiana, God spoke to me to get up early in the mornings and to walk a mile radius around our church. He instructed me to bless everything within that mile of the church and to pray against the strongholds of the Enemy within that area. One such stronghold was an adult bookstore. Not only did it have books, videos, magazines and adult toys, but it also had several video booths where a lot of other things went on that I won't mention. Every morning when I walked and prayed, I would stop and lay my hands on that building and pray against the Enemy's stronghold in the name of Jesus. Does that kind of thing really work? Within a few months, the health department came in and permanently closed down the adult bookstore.

Coincidence? I don't think so. James 5:16 says, "The effectual fervent prayer of a righteous man availeth much." God governs earth according to the prayers of His people. He is anxiously waiting for you and me to exercise the weapon of prayer, so that the His kingdom can be advanced on earth.

Fasting. This is the last offensive weapon I will mention, even though I am sure there are others as well. Referring to a particular kind of stronghold or fortress—that is, evil or demonic spirits— Jesus told His disciples on one occasion, only by prayer and fasting could this kind "come forth" (Mark 9:29).

Over the years, I have learned to discern when Satan has issued an all-out assault on my family, the church or me. My experience has been that it usually comes in waves or in seasons. My response to his assailment is always the same, more prayer combined with fasting.

I remember a time in my early 30s when I would get these excruciating sinus headaches every day at about 1 o'clock in the afternoon. They were accompanied by sinus drainage that was almost as unbearable as the headaches. When it would hit, I would respond by taking several Excedrin sinus pills and lie down for a couple of hours. After about a year of headaches and a couple of trips to the doctor, I knew it was an attack from Satan—a spirit of infirmity. His strategy was clear, God was blessing me and multiplying our church and our ministry throughout the city, and the attack was meant to discourage me and tear down my faith.

Finally, I reached a place of "Peniel" in my life. I knew I had to get away and have a face-to-face encounter with Almighty God. So I checked into a motel for three days with my Bible and a couple changes of clothes. I was determined that when I checked out, I would be healed. During that three-day period, I fasted, prayed, read God's Word and experienced spiritual warfare like I never knew was possible. The last night I was there, I had an experience that in some measure resembled Jacob's (see Genesis 32). During my praying and trying to sleep in the early hours of the morning, something like a heavy weight lifted from me. I knew when I awakened the next morning I was healed. I drove back to my home praising and thanking God. It's been over 10 years, and I have never experienced one sinus headache since that time.

When God Is on Your Side, You Can't Lose

How do we develop discernment in our personal lives and in our children? It starts with being controlled by the Spirit of God, knowing and obeying the truth, building a strong defense, and going on the offensive. Your family doesn't have to be sucked in by today's song crafters. Satan will tell you your kids will rebel no matter what you do and end up going the way of the culture. But that's a lie. Remember, if Satan's mouth is moving, he's lying to you. Receive the vision of God for your children's lives and do your best to teach and model discernment daily. As you sow, God will provide a great harvest in their lives in His season.

DISCUSSION QUESTIONS

1. Discuss the need for developing and practicing discernment in your home. Evaluate yourself in the following areas:

    a. Being controlled by the Spirit

    b. Knowing and Obeying the Truth

    c. Building a Strong Defense

    d. Going on the Offensive

The Home Crafters

Chapter Ten

Of all the influences in a young person's life, the family still ranks as the most influential force in our culture. Even in spite of the diversity of families today, no other institution or body directly crafts and shapes a child like a family. Thankfully, the majority of Americans still believe that the traditional family unit is by far the best and most effective family model in raising children. However, this is being questioned and tested today by some who feel that the traditional family structure has failed and other family models may be more effective. These individuals, organizations and movements, which I call the *home crafters*, believe that the modern concept of family must be redefined and expanded so that no particular kind of family should be discriminated against.

In this chapter, I address how the family is being redefined, how these changes are affecting children, and what the real reason behind the movement to redefine the family is.

A Major Societal Shift

Over the past three decades, cohabitation, divorce, single-parent homes, same-sex couples, and people living alone have dramatically increased while traditional two-parent families have shown a steady decline over that same period. In fact, according to the 2000 census, people living alone outnumbered traditional "married-with-children" families. At the same time, the number of households with "unmarried partners" increased a whopping 72 percent. Since 1960, cohabiting couples have grown 1,000 percent in the U.S., with over 4.7 million couples currently cohabiting. Now, half of all Americans ages 35 to 39 have lived with someone outside of marriage, according to researcher Larry Bumpass. Make no mistake: we are seeing a major societal shift take place.

Why the seismic changes? Demographers cite several reasons. The first is divorce. They say divorce rates are at historically high levels. They also point to research that shows that people are postponing and even forgoing marriage. The majority of today's busters and bridgers have never seen a successful, thriving marriage, mainly because they have become so scarce. Then, when you consider the media's dire public-relations campaign that seems to follow marriage, why would we expect marriage to look attractive to our children?

As marriage goes, so goes the family. As the family goes, so goes the culture. No culture has ever survived the breakdown of the home. Focus on the Family director Dr. James Dobson recently told his audience, "When marriage goes down, the family goes down; when the family goes down, the country goes down; and when the country goes down, Western civilization goes down. Everything [hinges] on marriage." The latest and possibly the greatest threat to marriage and the family is the legalization of gay marriage. The ramifications of legalized gay marriage could literally mean the death of the family as we have known it and the way God has designed it. Nonetheless, the majority of society today merely yawns at such a possibility. The secular media responds with its usual skepticism, asking, "Well, so what?" Why shouldn't the family, which they see as outmoded and irrelevant, be broadened and modernized? What harm could possibly be done by yielding to the demands of gays and lesbians?

'Gay Marriage: Why Would It Affect Me?'

In Dr. James Dobson's April 2004 newsletter, he refers to a column in the *Dallas Morning News* written by columnist Steve Blow, titled "Gay Marriage: Why Would It Affect Me?"

Dr. Dobson states, "[Steve] Blow said he had read one of my recent letters on this subject (same-sex marriage) and disagreed emphatically with my perspective. He wrote: "When opponents talk about the 'defense of marriage,' they lose me. James Dobson's Focus on the Family just sent out a mailer to 2.5 million homes saying: 'The homosexual activists' movement is poised to administer a devastating and potentially fatal blow to the traditional family.' And I say, 'Huh?' How does anyone's pledge of love and commitment turn into a fatal blow to families?"

Dr. Dobson responds by writing that people like Mr. Blow many times seem committed to "political correctness," along with others who hide in places where logic and facts cannot penetrate. Dobson then offered 10 powerful, factual arguments against gay marriage.

1. The implications for children in a world of decaying families are profound. A recent article in the *Weekly Standard* described how the advent of legally sanctioned gay unions in Scandinavian countries has already destroyed the institution of marriage, where half of today's children are born out of wedlock. It is predicted now, based on demographic trends in this country, that more than half of the babies born in the 1990s will spend at least part of their childhood in single-parent homes. Social scientists have been surprisingly consistent in warning against this fractured family. If it continues, almost every child will have several "moms" and "dads," perhaps six or eight "grandparents," and dozens of half-siblings. It will be a world where little boys and girls are shuffled from pillar to post in an ever-changing pattern of living arrangements—where huge numbers of them will be raised in foster-care homes or living on the street (as millions do in other countries all over the world today). Imagine an environment where nothing is stable and where people think primarily about themselves and their own self-preservation.

The apostle Paul described a similar society in Romans 1, which addressed the epidemic of homosexuality that was rampant in the ancient world and especially in Rome at that time. He wrote, "They have become filled with every kind of wickedness, evil, greed and depravity. They are full of envy, murder, strife, deceit and malice. They are gossips, slanderers, God-haters, insolent, arrogant and boastful; they invent ways of doing evil; they disobey their parents; they are senseless, faithless, heartless, ruthless" (vv. 29-31, *NIV*). It appears likely now that the demise of families will accelerate this type of decline dramatically, resulting in a chaotic culture that will be devastating to children.

2. The introduction of legalized gay marriages will lead inexorably to polygamy and other alternatives to one-man, one-woman unions. In Utah, polygamist Tom Green, who claims five wives, is citing *Lawrence v. Texas* as the legal authority for his appeal. This past January, a Salt Lake City civil rights attorney filed a federal lawsuit on behalf of another couple wanting to engage in legal polygamy. Their justification? *Lawrence v. Texas*. The ACLU of Utah has actually suggested that the state will "have to step up to prove that a polygamous relationship is detrimental to society"—as opposed to the polygamists having to prove that plural marriage is not harmful to the culture. Do you see how the game is played? Despite 5,000 years of history, the burden now rests on you and me to prove that polygamy is unhealthy. The ACLU went on to say that the nuclear family "may not be necessarily the best model." Indeed, Justice Antonin Scalia warned of this likelihood in his statement for the minority in the Lawrence case. It took less than six months for his prediction to become reality.

Why will gay marriage set the table for polygamy? Because there is no place to stop once the Rubicon has been crossed. Historically, the definition of marriage has rested on a bedrock of tradition, legal precedent, theology and the overwhelming support of the people. After the introduction of marriage between homosexuals, however, it will be supported by nothing more substantial than the opinion of a single judge or by a black-robed panel of justices. After they have done their wretched work, the family will consist of little more than someone's interpretation of "rights." Given that unstable legal climate, it is certain that some self-possessed judge, somewhere, will soon rule that three men and one woman can marry. Or five and two, or four and four. Who will be able to deny them that right? The guarantee is implied, we will be told, by the Constitution. Those who disagree will continue to be seen as hate-mongers and bigots. (Indeed, those charges are already being leveled against those of us who espouse biblical values!) How about group marriage, or marriage between relatives, or marriage between adults and children? How about marriage between a man and his donkey? Anything allegedly linked to "civil rights" will be doable. The legal underpinnings for marriage will have been destroyed.

3. An even greater objective of the homosexual movement is to end the state's compelling interest in marital relationships altogether. After marriages have been redefined, divorces will be obtained instantly, will not involve a court, and will take on the status of a driver's license or a hunting permit. With the family out of the way, all rights and privileges of marriage will accrue to gay and lesbian partners without the legal entanglements and commitments heretofore associated with it.

4. With the legalization of homosexual marriage, every public school in the nation will be required to teach that this perversion is the moral equivalent of traditional marriage between a man and a woman. Textbooks, even in conservative states, will have to depict man/man and woman/woman relationships, and stories written for children as young as elementary school, or even kindergarten, will have to give equal space to homosexuals.

5. From that point forward, courts will not be able to favor a traditional family involving one man and one woman over a homosexual couple in matters of adoption. Children will be placed in homes with parents representing only one sex on an equal basis with those having a mom and a dad. The prospect of

131

fatherless and motherless children will not be considered in the evaluation of eligibility. It will be the law.

6. Foster-care parents will be required to undergo "sensitivity training" to rid themselves of bias in favor of traditional marriage, and will have to affirm homosexuality in children and teens.

7. How about the impact on Social Security if there are millions of new dependents that will be entitled to survivor benefits? It will amount to billions of dollars on an already overburdened system. And how about the cost to American businesses? Unproductive costs mean fewer jobs for those who need them. Are state and municipal governments to be required to raise taxes substantially to provide health insurance and other benefits to millions of new "spouses and other dependents"?

8. Marriage among homosexuals will spread throughout the world, just as pornography did after the Nixon Commission declared obscene material "beneficial" to mankind. Almost instantly, the English-speaking countries liberalized their laws against smut. America continues to be the fountainhead of filth and immorality, and its influence is global. The point is that numerous leaders in other nations are watching to see how we will handle the issue of homosexuality and marriage. Only two countries in the world have authorized gay marriage to date—the Netherlands and Belgium. Canada is leaning in that direction, as are numerous European countries. Dr. Darrell Reid, president of Focus on the Family Canada, told me two weeks ago that his country is carefully monitoring the United States to see where it is going. If we take this step off a cliff, the family on every continent will splinter at an accelerated rate. Conversely, our U.S. Supreme Court has made it clear that it looks to European and Canadian law in the interpretation of our Constitution. What an outrage! That should have been grounds for impeachment, but the Congress, as usual, remained passive and silent.

9. Perhaps most important, the spread of the Gospel of Jesus Christ will be severely curtailed. The family has been God's primary vehicle for evangelism since the beginning. Its most important

assignment has been the propagation of the human race and the handing down of the faith to our children. Malachi 2:15 reads, referring to husbands and wives, "Has not the Lord made them one? In flesh and spirit they are his. And why one? Because he was seeking godly offspring. So guard yourself in your spirit, and do not break faith with the wife of your youth" (*NIV*). That responsibility to teach the next generation will never recover from the loss of committed, God-fearing families. The younger generation and those yet to come will be deprived of the Good News, as has already occurred in France, Germany and other European countries. Instead of providing for a father and mother, the advent of homosexual marriage will create millions of motherless children and fatherless kids. This is morally wrong, and is condemned in Scripture. Are we now going to join the Netherlands and Belgium to become the third country in the history of the world to "normalize" and legalize behavior that has been prohibited by God himself? Heaven help us if we do!

10. The culture war will be over, and I fear, the world may soon become "as it was in the days of Noah" (Matthew 24:37, *NIV*). This is the climactic moment in the battle to preserve the family, and future generations hang in the balance.

Redefining the Family: How It Affects the Children

I heard Josh McDowell say in a radio interview once, "The way a culture treats its children is the way the children will grow up and treat their culture."

In her book *Love and Economics*, Jennifer Roback Morse tells us there's an "impressive body of evidence" pointing to the difficulties faced by kids raised in single-parent homes and step-families. On average they complete fewer years of schooling and are more likely to "commit delinquent acts" and abuse alcohol and drugs than kids growing up in intact families. The impact of growing up in a single-parent home is well documented by research. Children are more likely to drop out of school, become sexually active and exhibit anxiety. These are just some of the consequences of kids being raised in single-parent homes, you name the problem and chances are high that it's more likely to occur in single-parent homes and in step-families than in two-parent homes.

While many single-parent families try to do their best for kids under adverse situations, there is another trendy kind of family that is making a disastrous impact upon the lives of millions of children—I am speaking of children being raised in "unmarried partner" homes. While the unmarried mom and dad may look like the average married couple, pairs living together, lacking formal long-term commitments have been found more likely to create problems for kids. Sociologists cite that children have a greater likelihood of experiencing emotional problems along with a greater chance of being abused by a live-in parent. For example: a cohabiting boyfriend is 30 times more likely to abuse a child than a father married to a child's mother. The Family Violence Research Program at the University of New Hampshire, the nation's leading institution studying domestic violence, finds that the overall rate of violence for cohabiting couples is twice as high as for married couples, and the overall rate for "severe" violence is nearly five times as high.

Annually, millions of children are born or moved into families where the mom and dad's commitment to each other is unstable. Their fundamental agreement is based upon a conditional commitment: "I'll stick with you as long as things go well. But if it gets rough, I might take off." Children that live with unmarried parents are deprived of the security that comes from knowing their parents have pledged themselves to each other for a lifetime. To make matters worse, an alarming 75 percent of all children born to cohabiting parents will experience their parents' separation before they reach age 16. Only about one-third of children born to married parents face a similar fate.

Is It Really About the Children?

Considering the higher rates of abuse, drug usage, sexual activity, emotional problems, and high school dropouts among children that come from single-parent and unmarried parents families, why are Americans choosing to forsake the traditional family structure of two married parents? We say we love our kids. We say we want the best for them. Yet, fewer and fewer American adults are choosing to stay together for the sake of their children. Why?

There is an answer, and it isn't a great mystery. We have become a culture bent on self-gratification. The number one deciding factor now for many is "What's best for me?" or "What will make me happy?" Personal autonomy has become the one value that trumps everything else. We care more about individual rights then we do about our children.

Newsweek recently ran a cover story entitled, "The Secret Lives of Wives." The feature article detailed personal stories in the current trend of working moms with children that are having extra-marital affairs. The article went on to say that infidelity among married women is becoming as widespread as infidelity among married men. Most sociologists agree that this latest trend is unprecedented in American culture. The explanation given for what the *Newsweek* story called the "new infidelity" was inattentive husbands preoccupied with their work, wives who are becoming increasingly more active outside the home, and women who grew up as teenagers in the promiscuous 70's and experimented with sex involving one or more relationships.

In pastoral counseling sessions, when I ask husbands or wives, "Why did you leave your spouse?" I get answers like, *I woke up one morning and just thought, I don't want to be married anymore*, or *I deserve better*, or *I just decided I needed to do this for me*. Ravi Zacharias said, "The reason we have a crisis in our gender relationships is that we would rather be served than serve. We would rather be the head than the feet." Call it self-indulgence, hedonism, self-pity, pleasure-seeking—however you diagnose it, it is a rampant plague that is sweeping the culture today.

The apostle Paul prophesied nearly 2,000 years ago that self-gratification would abound in a future time: "Remember that there will be difficult times in the last days. People will be selfish, greedy, boastful, and conceited; they will be insulting, disobedient to their parents, ungrateful, and irreligious; they will be unkind, merciless, slanderers, violent, and fierce; they will hate the good; they will be treacherous, reckless, and swollen with pride; they will love pleasure rather than God" (2 Timothy 3:1-4, *GNB*).

The Scheme of the Wicked One

The Bible reminds us in Ephesians 6:11, 12, "Put on all the armor that God gives you, so that you will be able to stand up against the Devil's evil tricks. For we are not fighting against human beings but against the wicked spiritual forces in the heavenly world, the rulers, authorities, and cosmic powers of this dark age" (*GNB*). The plan behind redefining the family or the destruction of the traditional family was devised by Satan and his cohorts. His plan is simply to bring into bondage as many people as he can to generational and emotional satanic strongholds, especially today's youth culture. He knows that if he can keep them in spiritual darkness, he can keep the gospel light hidden from them.

Paul wrote in 2 Corinthians 4:3-4, "But if our gospel be hid, it is hid to them that are lost: in whom the god of this world hath blinded the minds of them which believe not, lest the light of the glorious gospel of Christ, who is the image of God, should shine unto them" (*GNB*).

For the last year in our church, we have been sponsoring homogeneous "Encounter Weekends," which is a part of the G-12 (Government of the Twelve) model. As the leadership of our church has attended and conducted these weekend ministries, I have been amazed at the strongholds and bondages in Christians' lives. I am referring to generational sins and emotional wounds that have been there for years, even decades; physical and sexual abuse, emotional scars, and attitudes that have been suppressed for years that keeps Christians from being free in Christ and controlled by His Holy Spirit.

I have come to the conclusion that before we (the church) can reach the harvest of lost souls and do real ministry, we must be set free of Satan's bondages that are hiding the gospel light in the very ones Christ has entrusted to let His light shine so the world can see. How can we "give the light of the knowledge of the glory of God in the face of Jesus Christ" (2 Corinthians 4:6), if that light has become darkened by strongholds of the Enemy? Many of the worshipers in our churches today were children in the '70s and '80s. They sit in church pews by the millions bearing scars from divorce, abuse, drugs, abortion, alcohol, the occult—you name it, they have experienced it.

This is supposed to be the victorious, overcoming, triumphant church! Has the devil crippled families to the point where there is no hope for the families of the future, the church, and maybe our civilization? Is there an antithesis to the Enemy's malicious attacks and ravages on our homes? And if so, where do we begin?

DISCUSSION QUESTIONS

1. Discuss Josh McDowell's comment, "The way culture treats its children is the way the children will grow up and treat their culture."

2. How has the decline of the family impacted the church? Is the effectiveness of the family tied to the effectiveness of the church?

Countering the Home Crafters: *Ensuring God's Blessing for the Family*

Chapter Eleven

I once heard a story about a cynic sitting under a nut tree, carrying on a one-sided argument with God. He was questioning God's creative designs, sarcastically poking fun at the disparities in the universe. "Lord," he said, "how is it that You made such a large tree to hold such a tiny nut? And yet You made such a small, tender plant to hold such a big and hefty watermelon!"

About that time, a nut suddenly fell from the tree and landed squarely on his head. After a pause, he mumbled, "Thank God, that wasn't a watermelon."

Like the cynic questioning the watermelon vine and the nut tree, God's creative patterns are often beyond man's understanding. However, man makes a grave error when he attempts to rework God's original designs. God, at creation, laid down His perfect plan for the family. God said that a family should originate with *a man who separates from his father and his mother, cleaves to his wife, and the two become one flesh* (Genesis 2:24). Throughout the Bible, God instructs the man and the woman concerning how they are to perform their roles as husband and wife and, upon having children, as father and mother. God leaves no stone unturned. In the Bible, He provides all the information necessary for successful marriages and fruitful families.

Well, then, how did we get it so fouled up? What went wrong with the family? The answer: the devil. Now by this time, everyone who doesn't believe in a devil and in demons has probably already stopped reading this book. But he is the father of lies, and he is the author of confusion. When you give him the opportunity, he will divide and destroy anything and everything, including your marriage and your family. He specializes in wreaking havoc. As already stated, he knows that if he can bring down families, he can bring down churches, communities and nations.

So how do we counter the cultural home crafters that Satan is using to destroy the family? Is it too late? Where do we begin?

God Himself Is Raising Up a Standard

Isaiah 59:19 says, "So shall they fear the name of the Lord from the west, and his glory from the rising of the sun. When the enemy shall come in like a flood, the Spirit of the Lord shall lift up a standard against him."

Unquestionably, God is raising up a standard to keep at bay the work of Satan today. Particularly, over the last 25 years, God has raised up one ministry after another that edifies the family. Ministries such as James Dobson's Focus on the Family, the American Family Radio Network, and Promise Keepers have served as tools in the hands of Almighty God to pull down the strongholds of the Enemy against the family.

In 1997, I participated, along with over a million other men, in the Promise Keepers' Men's Rally in Washington, D.C. I have never sensed the presence of Almighty God more than I did during that glorious event. Something happened in the spiritual realm on that day in America. God honored the prayers of heads of families who came together to repent on behalf of the sins of the nation.

Is God still raising up a standard today after 9/11? Absolutely, God's Spirit is moving in churches throughout America that long after the heart of God. He has set His Spirit upon His church, He has chosen His church to bring good news to the poor, to proclaim liberty to the captives and recovery of sight to the blind, to set the oppressed free, and to announce that the time has come when the Lord will save His people (Luke 4:18).

God has a true and faithful church today in America, and God is moving mightily through His church to bring healing, deliverance and restoration to families. I know a lot of Christians who are critical of God's church. The church is an easy target. We the members are weak and vulnerable. Too many preachers and laity spend their time talking about what the church needs to do rather than doing what needs to be done.

But God has not given up on His church. The true, alive church is ministering to families. All God requires is that we His people, who are called by His name, humble ourselves, pray, seek His face, and turn from our wicked ways. Then, He says, "I will hear from heaven, and will forgive their sin, and will heal their land" (2 Chronicles 7:14).

How to Get God's Blessing for Your Family

Having God's blessing and favor upon your life, your family, your church, your occupation, and even your community, is paramount. You can pray for it, long for it, confess and claim it all you want, but it only comes by doing two things: (1) listening obediently to the voice of God and (2) with your whole heart obeying His commandments. As easy as it may seem, if you will put into practice these two things daily, you will experience the blessing and favor of Almighty God.

I want you to read for yourself what God says He will do for you if you will just listen to Him and obey Him:

And it shall come to pass, *if thou shalt hearken diligently unto the voice of the Lord* thy God, to observe *and to do all his commandments* which I command thee this day, that the Lord thy God will set thee on high above all nations of the earth: and *all these blessings shall come on thee, and overtake thee*, if thou shalt hearken unto the voice of the Lord thy God. Blessed shalt thou be in the city, and blessed shalt thou be in the field. Blessed shall be the fruit of thy body, and the fruit of thy ground, and the fruit of thy cattle, the increase of thy kine, and the flocks of thy sheep. Blessed shall be thy basket and thy store. Blessed shalt thou be when thou comest in, and blessed shalt thou be when thou goest out. The Lord shall cause thine enemies that rise up against thee to be smitten before thy face: they shall come out against thee one way, and flee before thee seven ways. The Lord shall command the blessing upon thee in thy storehouses, and in all that thou settest thine hand unto; and he shall bless thee in the land which the Lord thy God giveth thee. The Lord shall establish thee an holy people unto himself, as he hath sworn unto thee, if thou shalt keep the commandments of the Lord thy God, and walk in his ways. And all people of the earth shall see that thou art called by the name of the Lord; and they shall be afraid of thee. And the Lord shall make thee plenteous in goods, in the fruit of thy body, and in the fruit of thy cattle, and in the fruit of thy ground, in the land which the Lord sware unto thy fathers to give thee. The Lord shall open unto thee his good treasure, the heaven to give the rain unto thy land in his season, and to bless all the work of thine hand: and thou shalt lend unto many nations, and thou shalt not borrow. And the Lord shall make thee the head, and not the tail; and thou shalt be above only, and thou shalt not be beneath; if that thou hearken unto the commandments of the Lord thy God, which I command thee this day, to observe and to do them.—Deuteronomy 28:1-13

Doesn't that make you want to rejoice! God says these blessings shall *come on you, and overtake you*. I love that thought! You might wonder, Is God saying that to me? And the answer is *yes* . . . if you are listening to His voice and obeying His commands. God wants to bless His people. God really does want His people *to be the head and not the tail*. God wants to bless you, your family, your future generations, your church and your community. He truly desires for His people to be exalted throughout the earth.

My father retired from pastoring a few years ago due to Parkinson's disease. My dad and mom pastored churches throughout Indiana for over 25 years. They never drew a big salary, and they never pastored a large congregation, but they were faithful to the call of God upon their lives. I heard my dad recently tell of a time when he was doing some yard work around a church he was pastoring in the early '90s. He said he was praying for his children and his grandchildren when God showed him a vision of how he was going to bless and make his family fruitful for generations to come. God assured him that because of his and my mother's faithfulness and obedience, a legacy of righteousness would follow him as far as his grandchildren's children.

I have truly benefited from my parents' obedience to God. Even though my wife and I have faced our share of trials, they don't show up on the radar screen compared to the blessings of God upon our family. Nonetheless, as sure as God's blessing comes upon and overtakes those that are obedient, so too does the curse of God come upon and overtake those that live in disobedience. I know it's not popular today to talk about being cursed of God. People in our culture only think of curses in reference to witches, wizards or evil in general. But the Bible is very clear that our sinful disobedience can bring a curse upon on us, upon our family, and even upon our church, as well as our community. God doesn't just look the other way when we willfully disobey Him. Like a loving father, he wants us to learn from our disobedience. Therefore, God allows curses to come upon the disobedient so that we might humble ourselves, repent and walk in obedience.

Look now at Deuteronomy 28:15-25:

But it shall come to pass, if thou wilt not hearken unto the voice of the Lord thy God, to observe to do all his commandments and his statutes which I command thee this day; that all these curses shall come upon thee, and overtake thee: Cursed shalt thou be in the city, and cursed shalt thou be in the field. Cursed shall be thy basket and thy store. Cursed shall be the fruit of thy body, and the fruit of thy land, the increase of thy kine, and the flocks of thy sheep. Cursed shalt thou be when thou comest in, and cursed shalt thou be when thou goest out. The Lord shall send upon thee cursing, vexation, and rebuke, in all that thou settest thine hand unto for to do, until thou be destroyed, and until thou perish quickly; because of the wickedness of thy doings, whereby thou hast forsaken me. The Lord shall make the pestilence cleave unto thee, until he have consumed thee from off the land, whither thou goest to possess it. The Lord shall smite thee with a consumption, and with a fever, and with an inflammation, and with an extreme burning, and with the sword, and with blasting, and with mildew; and they shall pursue thee until thou perish. And thy heaven that is over thy head shall be brass, and the earth that is under thee shall be iron. The Lord shall make the rain of thy land powder and dust: from heaven shall it come down upon thee, until thou be destroyed. The Lord shall cause thee to be smitten before thine enemies: thou shalt go out one way against them, and flee seven ways before them: and shalt be removed into all the kingdoms of the earth.

Enough already! Why would anyone choose to live that kind of life? How about you? What about your family? Don't you want your family to know the blessings and the favor of God rather than live under the curse? Then begin to hear God's voice and walk in obedience. Surrender your life to Jesus Christ and experience His blessing and His favor.

God Is Looking for Abrahams Today

I believe God is still looking for Abrahams today—men and women who will unreservedly obey God, no matter what He says. From all Scriptural indication, Abraham was a first-generation follower of God—Jehovah, the Lord. The only thing that separated him from his father and his father's forefathers was that Abraham heard God's voice and obeyed. Hebrews 11:8-12, says: "By faith Abraham, when he was called to go out into a place which he should after receive for an inheritance, obeyed; and he went out, not knowing whither he went. By faith he sojourned in the land of promise, as in a strange country, dwelling in tabernacles with Isaac and Jacob, the heirs with him of the same promise: For he looked for a city which hath foundations, whose builder and maker is God. Through faith also Sara herself received strength to conceive seed, and was delivered of a child when she was past age, because she judged him faithful who had promised. Therefore sprang there even of one, and him as good as dead, so many as the stars of the sky in multitude, and as the sand which is by the sea shore innumerable." *(KJV)*

As Abraham listened and obeyed God, God's blessings *overtook* him and his wife, Sarah, and his son, Isaac, and grandson, Jacob. God began a legacy of righteousness starting with Abraham. Does this mean that Isaac and Jacob could live in disobedience to God and still have everything go smoothly? Not exactly, but it does mean that God's blessing and favor followed them because of Abraham's obedience.

God is looking for men today that will wholeheartedly listen to His voice and obey Him. He will do the rest. All He wants from us is total consecration. Will you be the flame that ignites future generations of righteousness for your family? Are you ready to be the Abraham that God will use to bring about His blessing and favor upon your children, grandchildren and their children?

My father is an Abraham. He was the first one in his family to be converted to Christ. Of all places, he committed his life to Christ in the restroom of a hospital. Previously, he had attended church just a few times, but it took his firstborn son slipping into a comatose condition for him to turn his life over to Jesus Christ. As he tells it, "I knelt in the floor of the hospital restroom and told God that if He would raise up my son, I would serve Him for the rest of my life. God brought my son out of the coma the next day, and I have served Him since." And just in case you were wondering, I was the son that God miraculously healed.

A Final Word to Men

So often, as the father goes, so goes the family. It is God's plan for men to lead their families. Ephesians 5:23 says, "The husband provides leadership to his wife the way Christ does to his church, not by domineering but by cherishing" (*MSG*). When men lead and love their wives and children as Christ does the church, God will bless and prosper families, churches and communities. Every church I have pastored that was strong and fruitful had men who were godly leaders in their homes.

More than at any time in the history of our nation, there is a need for godly men to disciple and mentor young men. The majority of young men in our culture have never had a positive male role model in their lives. Sadly, the same can be said about men in the Christian community, the church. Young men today have been deceived and confused by today's culture crafters. They have been taught that being a man is all about watching football, or how much beer you can drink, or whom you can score with, or how much money you can make, or how many toys you own. Is it any wonder that real women, beautiful inside and out, are turned off by this kind of man?

Men by their very god-given responsibilities are called to be leaders. John Maxwell says leadership is influence. When you have been given influence, you must lead. It's not an option; it's a mandate given by the Creator. The question is not "Will you lead?" but "How will you lead?"

God has called us as men to lead like Christ. He is the greatest leader known to man. He exemplified servant leadership when he walked on earth, and He is still leading His church today while sitting at the right hand of the Father. Through the power of His Spirit, we can love and cherish our wives like Christ does the church. By submitting to Christ's leadership in our own lives, we too can successfully lead our families and experience God's blessing and favor for generations to come.

DISCUSSION QUESTIONS

1. Is God's blessing and favor upon your family? If so, describe His blessings and favor upon your life, family, and career? If not, what do you believe is keeping God's blessing and favor from overtaking you?

2. Discuss mentoring as seen in the New and Old Testament. Are you presently being mentored by someone or are you mentoring someone? Discuss the need for mentoring in the church today.

The Christ Crafter

Chapter Twelve

I said to myself, "Let's go for it—experiment with pleasure, have a good time!" But there was nothing to it, nothing but smoke.

What do I think of the fun-filled life? Insane! Inane! My verdict on the pursuit of happiness? Who needs it?

With the help of a bottle of wine and all the wisdom I could muster, I tried my level best to penetrate the absurdity of life. I wanted to get a handle on anything useful we mortals might do during the years we spend on this earth.

Oh, I did great things: built houses, planted vineyards, designed gardens and parks and planted a variety of fruit trees in them, made pools of water to irrigate the groves of trees.

I bought slaves, male and female, who had children, giving me even more slaves; then I acquired large herds and flocks, larger than any before me in Jerusalem.

I piled up silver and gold, loot from kings and kingdoms. I gathered a chorus of singers to entertain me with song, and—most exquisite of all pleasures—voluptuous maidens for my bed.

Oh, how I prospered! I left all my predecessors in Jerusalem far behind, left them behind in the dust. What's more, I kept a clear head through it all.

Everything I wanted I took—I never said no to myself. I gave in to every impulse, held back nothing. I sucked the marrow of pleasure out of every task—my reward to myself for a hard day's work!

Then I took a good look at everything I'd done, looked at all the sweat and hard work. But when I looked, I saw nothing but smoke. Smoke and spitting into the wind. There was nothing to any of it. Nothing.—Ecclesiastes 2:1-11, *The Message*

These words were written by King Solomon, whose father, David, was an immensely popular and powerful king of Israel. Solomon and the current boomer generation (born between 1946 and 1964) have much in common. Both Solomon and today's boomers had fathers who were successful war heroes. David, who had defeated Goliath, the Philistine, and was known as a mighty warrior as well as a successful king. The fathers of boomers are known for bringing an end to World War II by defeating Hitler and Nazism and dropping the atomic bombs. Both David and the fathers of boomers brought wealth, peace, strength and prominence to their respective countries.

Like Solomon, boomers have fathers that gave them opportunity for prosperity, freedom, education and status. The boomers' parents, notoriously tagged as the "greatest generation" by Tom Brokaw (born between 1922-1945) are responsible for creating affluence in America through their hard work and entrepreneurship. As a result, they encouraged their children to enjoy the prosperity, become educated, and make a better future for themselves and their children. Consequently, the '60s saw millions of boomers flock to America's higher institutions of learning, as their parents had hoped for.

Robert H. Bork, former solicitor general and attorney general of the United States, wrote, "The baby boomers were a generation so large (79 million still living by 1974) that they formed their own culture rather than being assimilated into the existing one. The culture boomers formed was, as is natural for adolescents, opposed to that of their parents."

The boomer's new culture became a counterculture that basically argued and resisted the traditional culture of their parents. They were a coddled generation that valued personal comfort, convenience and individualism. In Judge Bork's book *Slouching Toward Gomorrah,* he explains that one of the characteristics of the '60s generation was boredom due to the absence of economic pressure and, in his words, "the assumption that there would never be want in their future." Judge Bork writes, "Boredom is a much underrated emotion. It is an emotion that is dangerous for individuals and for society because a lot of the cures are antisocial: alcohol, narcotics, cruelty, pornography, violence, zealotry in a political cause. Many of the sixties generation shopped that list."

The culture crafters of the '60s affirmed and incited individualistic attitudes that birthed both national and international student movements, radical ideas, revolts, violence and a short-lived revolution. Who were the culture crafters that influenced the boomers of the '60s? They were liberal university educators, student-led movements, radical politicians, leftist organizations, and rock music, all of which intensified the rebelliousness of the '60s youth.

By the early '70s, the '60s revolution as a movement had died out. However, its liberal ideology, attitudes and counterculture rebellion continued. Its influence is still felt within our universities, and its impact can be felt anywhere attitudes and opinions are expressed. Admittedly, today it is no longer considered a counterculture but a key part of our popular culture's liberal agenda. One *New York Times* editorial suggests, "The counterculture is [now] part of us, a legacy around which Americans can now unite, rather than allow themselves to be divided."

A Legacy of Emptiness

Solomon, after his pursuit of happiness and following his experimentation with all of his wine and wisdom, then did something that the majority of boomers have failed to do—he stepped back and took a long look at everything he had done. His conclusion, "When I looked, I saw nothing but smoke. Smoke and spitting into the wind. There was nothing to any of it. Nothing!" (Ecclesiastes 2:11, *The Message*).

After Solomon considered all he had accomplished, he calculated the total worth as zero. . . nothing. Solomon was honest enough to admit to himself that his earthly fortunes, knowledge, wisdom and accomplishments were of no internal or eternal value. In spite of his efforts, at the end of the day, the void and the emptiness in his inner man could never be filled.

Today's boomers have trouble owning up to the fact that many of their ideas, beliefs and individualistic attitudes birthed out the '60s helped fashion a culture that is now spiritually, morally and emotionally bankrupt. Many of the boomers, some of whom have now turned 50 can see that their children (the busters) are even more unimpressed and restless with the culture and its offerings. Like Solomon, busters have lived by the dictum "Let's go for it—experiment with pleasure, have a good time!" (Ecclesiastes 2:1, *MSG*). But now, many in the Buster generation is coming to the same realization that Solomon did: "There was nothing to it, nothing but smoke" (v. 11, *MSG*).

As a pastor, I see a constant stream of people in their 30s and 40s come into my church, repent of their sins and be wonderfully converted. From that moment, it's a joy to watch Christ change them into completely different people. They say things like "Everything seems so alive now," or "I don't worry anymore; I'm so happy now." And all of them say something like "My life has meaning now, a purpose. I feel so fulfilled."

Most of the people who are converted in our evangelical churches today have experienced nearly everything the world offers. Many are from broken homes, carrying all kinds of relational, emotional, financial and religious baggage. Their lifestyle of sin has led to some painful self-inflicted wounds in their lives. They come to Christ for healing, restoration, forgiveness and hope.

The quandary of the culture is that when its crafters finish shaping and molding the craft, it has no solution for the emptiness and the void that only the Creator can fill. The culture crafters can entertain, educate, entice, seduce and deceive, but they can't satisfy man's innate desire to know his Creator and to have fellowship with Him. The soul of man longs for it. The Spirit of God inflames it.

The Confrontation of Christ

Every man, woman and child will face a major confrontation at some time or at various times in their lives. This confrontation is initiated by Almighty God, the Creator. He has only one motive behind the confrontation—His great, infinite, unconditional love for His creation. "For God so loved the world, that he gave his only begotten Son, that whosoever believeth in him should not perish, but have everlasting life," (John 3:16).

When the culture shapes our thinking, our attitudes and our actions, the Bible calls it walking "according to the course of this world, according to the prince of the power of the air, the spirit that now worketh in the children of disobedience" (Ephesians 2:2). Satan is the prince of the power of the air. Our struggle is not with the culture crafters of our day (flesh and blood), "but against principalities, against powers, against the rulers of the darkness of this world, against spiritual wickedness in high places" (Ephesians 6:2). It's the devil and his cohorts who are giving the orders to the culture crafters, and they follow because they have been blinded and deceived by this world.

This is why God sent His Son, Jesus, into the world "to open their eyes, and to turn them from darkness to light, and from the power of Satan unto God, that they may receive forgiveness of sins, and inheritance among them which are sanctified [purified] by faith that is in me" (Acts 26:18). Did you digest all of that? This is what Jesus said to Saul (later known as Paul) when he appeared to him on the Damascus road. He said, *I have come to open people's blinded eyes, to bring them from darkness into light, to deliver them out of the power of Satan, so that they might ask for and obtain forgiveness of their sins, and be made pure and clean in me.*

As Jesus confronted Saul on the Damascus road, He will confront you. There is no way to avoid it. He confronts everyone, because "all have sinned, and come short of the glory of God" (Romans 3:23). He may have already confronted you, and if not, He will.

How does Jesus confront people? He confronts sinners by His Spirit. The Bible, in John 16:8-11, says His Spirit convicts, or convinces, of three things:

1. The Spirit convinces sinners of sin. Like an attorney of law, He works in our conscience, convincing us of the fact of our sin, of the fault of our sin, of the folly of our sin, and the filth of our sin. He shows us that our sin is repulsive to God and that the fruit of our sin is death, that is, eternal destruction. The Spirit demonstrates the depravity of the whole world, that all the world is guilty before God.

2. The Spirit convinces sinners "of righteousness, because I go to my Father, and you see me no more" (v. 10). The Spirit of God convinces the world of Christ's personal righteousness, showing us, by convicting us of sin, our need for righteousness—a justification that is from God, not established by ourselves.

3. The Spirit convinces by the judgment of the prince of this world (Satan), whom Christ disarmed at the Cross. It is the Holy Spirit who convinces us that Christ through His sinless life, His death, His resurrection and ascension has set all things in order, that *the prince of this world* is judged and expelled, and that Jesus Christ has all power and dominion. The Spirit convinces the world that all judgment is committed to Jesus Christ, that He is Lord of all, that He has broken the serpent's head and destroyed him who had the power of death and spoiled principalities. Finally, on that final Day of Judgment, Satan and all the enemies of Christ's gospel and kingdom will be reckoned with at last, for the devil is judged.

Confrontation + Change

As the Spirit of God convicts and convinces of sin, righteousness and judgment, it is then the responsibility of sinners to repent of their sins and turn their lives over to God. The Bible says that Saul on the Damascus road did not disobey the vision that he received from Christ (Acts 26:19), but according to the next verse, Acts 26:20, Paul practiced and preached three things:

1. **Repent of your sins.** Be sorry for them and confess them. The Greek word rendered "repent" means "to think differently." In other words, we ought to change our mind and change our ways.

2. **Turn to God.** Not only turn away from that which is evil, but also turn to that which is good. We must turn to God, in love and affection, and surrender our lives over to Him in daily obedience according to His Word.

3. **Do works worthy of repentance.** If we are going to profess repentance, we must practice it and be truly remorseful when we do sin. It isn't enough just to say we are sorry, but our actions that follow our profession should prove that we are truly sorry.

True repentance brings change or conversion. The Bible says that Peter, like Paul, preached, "Repent ye therefore, and be converted, that your sins may be blotted out, when the times of refreshing shall come from the presence of the Lord " (Acts 3:19). John the Baptist also came preaching repentance–especially, to the religious leaders of his time. Jesus, too, preached repentance during his ministry.

Repentance is not a onetime thing; it is something that should be practiced anytime we sin. If you are a Christian and you want to be continually changing into the image of Christ, if you want your sins constantly to be obliterated, if you want times of refreshing to come upon you from being in the presence of the Lord—then you should practice repentance! A lack of repentance brings stagnation, sinful living, and spiritual deadness. This is the reason why many of today's churches in America are spiritually dead, there is a lack of repentance by saints in the altars. God help the church to get back to preaching and practicing repentance!

If you do not profess to be a Christian, but you would like to be one, then simply do the three things that Paul preached: repent of your sins, turn to God, and do works worthy of repentance. Jesus Christ will change you too!

Confrontation + Change = Fullness

Several years ago, the Army Corps of Engineers built a reservoir on the Texas-Mexico border. They estimated it would take three years for it to fill. But a hurricane filled it up in one night! Just as swiftly, when Jesus comes into our lives, He fills the emptiness with His fullness. Colossians 2:9, 10 says, "For in him [Christ] dwelleth all the fulness of the Godhead bodily. And ye are complete in him, which is the head of all principality and power."

What does that fullness of Christ look like? One of Charles Spurgeon's devotionals gives us a beautiful description of Christ's fullness in the life of the believer:

- There is a *fullness* in Christ. There is a *fullness* of essential Deity, for in Him dwelleth all the *fullness* of the Godhead. . . . There is a *fullness* of atoning efficacy in His blood, for the blood of Jesus Christ, His Son, cleanseth us from all sin. . . . There is a *fullness* of justifying righteousness in His life, for "there is therefore now no condemnation to them that are in Christ Jesus. . . . There is a *fullness* of victory in His death, for through death He destroyed him that had the power of death, that is the devil.

- There is a *fullness* of efficacy in His resurrection from the dead, for by it we are begotten again unto a lively hope.

- There is a *fullness* of blessings of every sort and shape; a *fullness* of grace to pardon, of grace to regenerate, of grace to sanctify, of grace to preserve, and of grace to perfect.

- There is a *fullness* at all times . . . of comfort in affliction, of guidance in prosperity. A *fullness* of every divine attribute, of wisdom, of power, of love; a *fullness* which it were impossible to survey, much less to explore.

- It pleased the Father that in Him should all fullness dwell. Oh, what a *fullness* must this be of which all receive! Fullness, indeed, must there be when the stream is always flowing, and yet the well springs up as free, as rich, as full as ever.

- Come, believer, and get all thy need supplied; ask largely, and thou shalt receive largely, for this *fullness* is inexhaustible, and is treasured up where all the needy may reach it, even in Jesus, Immanuel—God with us.

Randy L. Ballard

Scrounge

During my pastoral ministry, I have been blessed to see Christ confront and change many people. One of my favorites is a man everyone called Scrounge, whose real name is Kent.

Before coming to Christ, Scrounge rode with an outlaw bike gang, and he did everything outlaw gangs do. Scrounge's wife, Santa (that's right, as in Claus), began attending our church because her brother and his family attended there. She would bring her little boy with her and would often request prayer for her husband to be saved. One night I visited them in their home, and he made it clear that he really didn't want to talk to "no preacher." Nonetheless, Santa was determined to see her husband saved. She constantly shared Christ with Scrounge along with his fellow gang members. Santa would even go to club parties with her husband and preach to them about hell, heaven and the coming of Jesus.

Santa wasn't alone in her prayers; she had a dad and mom who were, and still are, radically in love with Jesus Christ. Her dad, Noah (no, this really is a true story, and I am not changing their real names either), obeyed God like the ancient Noah. He never built an ark, but if God gave him the dimensions and said, "Build it," he wouldn't ask one question. Scrounge was surrounded by a praying wife and in-laws that were not intimidated by an outlaw gang, hell or devils. In reality, Scrounge never had a chance—it was just a matter of time.

One night, a friend at Scrounge's work invited him to attend a Carmen concert, a contemporary gospel singer. The Spirit of Almighty God got a hold on Scrounge that night, and he had a "Damascus road" confrontation with Jesus Christ. Scrounge showed up at my church shortly thereafter and publicly came forward and repented of his sins. At that point, the Spirit of God wonderfully cleansed Scrounge of his sins, and Jesus filled him with His fullness. Scrounge was a different man.

Immediately, Scrounge and I begin to meet on Thursday evenings after his work for discipleship. He was humble, hungry for God's Word, and anxious to grow in Christ. I later learned that he told God he would stay off his bike and not go around his club buddies until he felt like he could influence them for Christ. He didn't pick up a bike for nearly two years. Scrounge didn't want anything or anyone to distract him from his pursuit of Christ.

At the end of his first year in Christ, he expressed a desire to begin to share his testimony and to share the Word of God with men in jails and prisons. Since neither I nor the church had a prison or jail ministry, he and I traveled to Georgia to attend a conference for training in how to be most effective in jail and prison ministry. At that conference, Scrounge got hooked. He immediately went back home to Terre Haute and got involved in a ministry in counseling troubled boys. From there, the door opened for him to go into the nearby state penitentiary, where he counseled and held a worship service for inmates.

Twelve years later, Scrounge pastors an inner-city church, where God is saving and changing the lives of drug addicts, alcoholics and outlaw gang members. He conducts two church services on Sundays, and both are packed wall-to-wall. His church sponsors two coffee house outreaches that target people who are hurting and in need. Scrounge also is the founder of a biker ministry that now has chapters operating in states throughout the Midwest.

Scrounge still wears his hair long. He still wears his bike leathers most of the time. He still looks rough on the outside, and he still speaks with a gruff in his voice. But since his initial confrontation with God, he has never been the same. The Spirit of God changed him, turned him inside out, and filled him with the fullness of Christ.

The Culture or the Christ?

In Matthew 8:28-34, the story is told of Jesus' going into the territory of Gadara after He had crossed the Sea of Galilee by boat. Jesus was met by two men who had just come out of the caves where the dead were buried. The Bible says these men were unclothed and were possessed by demons. No one traveled the road because everyone in Gadara feared these fierce men.

When the men saw Jesus, the demons screamed, "What do you want with us, you Son of God? Have you come to punish us before the right time?" (v. 29, *GNB*). The demons then begged Jesus, "If you are going to drive us out, send us into that herd of pigs" (v. 31, *GNB*). So Jesus cast the demons out, and they entered into a herd of pigs causing them to run off a cliff into a lake, where the entire herd drowned.

In case you are wondering . . . when the pigs drowned, the demons came out and are still active somewhere today - undoubtedly, still driving people crazy! Dr. Luke records that the men from whom the demons were driven out were sitting at the feet of Jesus, clothed and in their right mind. But notice the reaction of the community: "And they were all afraid" (Luke 8:35, *GNB*).

"The men who had been taking care of the pigs ran away and went into the town, where they told the whole story and what had happened to the men with the demons. So everyone from the town went out to meet Jesus; and when they saw him, they begged him to leave their territory" (Matthew 8:33, 34, *GNB*).

This story set me to wondering why these people from Gadara would beg Jesus to leave. Everything He had done was good. He changed these men for the good, which was also good for their community—the people no longer were afraid of them. The only ones who suffered were the owners of the pigs and the pigs themselves, and everyone knows Jews detest swine anyway. So what did Jesus do that would justify the people's plea for His departure?

Like the community of Gadara, everyone has a choice to make. Will we choose Jesus and the all the good that He brings? Or will we side with the swine owners and the greed, self-indulgence and avarice they represent?

This is the decision facing our culture today. We can either let the truth in Christ craft our lives or be crafted by the lies and deception of the culture. If we choose the culture, we choose death and eternal destruction. If we choose Christ, we choose abundant life on this earth and life eternal in the world to come.

Have you made your choice? Will it be the culture or Christ the Savior for you?

DISCUSSION QUESTIONS

1. Discuss the emptiness and restlessness that seems to characterize our culture today. What does the boomer generation and Solomon have in common?

2. Have you experienced the changing power of Jesus Christ? Share with others how Christ first confronted you by His Spirit and changed you?

3. Is there any hope for our culture today? What is our responsibility as Christians?

Bibliography

- Connie Neal, *Walking Tall in Babylon*, (Colorado Springs, CO., WaterBrook Press, 2003).
- Gene Edward Veith, Ph.D., "No Room for Truth" at Focus on the Family's *Teachers Magazine*, *www.family.org.cforum. teachersmag.*
- Jim Leffel, "Our New Challenge: Postmodernism," in the *Death of Truth*, ed. Dennis McCallum (Minneapolis: Bethany House, 1996).
- Benno Muller-Hill, "Science, Truth, and Other Values," *Quarterly Review of Biology,* Volume 68, Number 3, (September 1993).
- Francis J. Beckwith and Gregory Koukl, *Relativism*, (Grand Rapids, MI., Baker Books, 1998).
- Ravi Zacharias weekly radio program, December 14, 2003.
- George Barna, *What Americans Believe,* (Ventura, CA., Regal Books, 1991).
- Neil Postman, *Amusing Ourselves to Death,* (New York, New York: Penguin Books, 1985).
- Daniel J. Boorstin, *The Americans: The Colonial Experience,* (New York: Vintage Books, 1958).
- Paul Schatzkin, "The Boy Who Invented Television," *www. farnovision.com.*
- Leonard Sweet, *Carpe Manana,* (Grand Rapids, MI., Zondervan, 2001).
- Focus on the Family's Youth Culture, "Power of the Media," *www.family.org.*

- "Mind Over Media," *www.family.org.*
- Michael Medved, "Kill Bill Mocks Innate Revulsion toward Cruelty," *USA Today*, October 22, 2003.
- "Sex and Violence in the Media Fact Sheet," *www.parentstv. org.*
- Marilyn Elias, "When Friends Talk, Teens Listen," *USA Today*, November 3, 2003.
- Steve Jordahl, "Infidelity Growing Because of Internet," (July 23, 2003) at Focus on the Family's CitzenLink, *www.family.org/ cforum.*
- Andy Butcher, "How One Man Unleashed the Porn Plague," *CHARISMA* magazine, November, 2003.
- "Pornography Statistics," *info@FamilySafeMedia.com.*
- Janet Kornblum, "Ad, TV shows target HIV/AIDS," *USA Today*, January 12, 2004.
- Matt Kaufman, "Sex, Lies, and MTV," *Boundless Webzine.*
- Kimberly Daniels, *Clean House—Strong House,* (Lake Mary, Florida: Charisma House, 2003).
- Peggy Noonan, "A Tough Roe," *Wall Street Journal*, January 23, 2003. Evan Thomas, "The War Over Gay Marriage," *Newsweek*, July 7, 2003.
- Dr. Bill Maier, "Homosexual Mentors for Fatherless Boys?" (February 20, 2003), at Focus on the Family's CitzenLink, www.family.org/cforum.
- Robert Bianco, "Programming beyond stereotypes," *USA Today*, December 26, 2003.
- Alessandra Stanley, "Women Having Sex, Hoping Men Tune In," *New York Times*, January 16, 2004.
- Steve Jordahl, "Gay Relationships Short-lived, Dutch Study Says," (July 29, 2003), at Focus on the Family's CitzenLink, www.family.org/cforum.
- Jeremy Deck, "My Father's Closet," *www.boundless.org/2000/ features.*
- C. Everett Koop, "A Physician Looks at Abortion," in *Thou Shalt Not Kill,* ed. Richard L. Ganz (New York: Crown Publishers, Inc., 1978).

- Steve Jordahl, "Planned Parenthood's Coffers Grow Fatter," December 16, 2003, *www.family.org.*
- Celeste McGovern, "A Citizen investigation: The sale of baby parts is big business in North America," *www.family.org/cforum/citizenmag/features.*
- John Calvin, *Commentaries on the Four Last Books of Moses,* trans. Charles William Bingham, 4 vols. (Grand Rapids: Wm. B. Eerdmans Publishing Co., 1950).
- Amy Stephens, "What Exactly Is 'Mature Teen Sex'?" CitzenLink, *www.family.org.* Amy Stephens, "Trust Your Kids, Not Condoms," CitzenLink, *www.family.org.*
- Focus on the Family Physicians Resource Council, U.S.A.
- Alan Bloom, *The Closing of the American Mind* (New York: Simon & Schuster, 1987).
- Richard J. Neuhaus, "The Public Square," *First Things,* December 1997.
- Kay Haugard, "Moral Judgment," *The Chronicle of Higher Education,* June 27, 1997.
- J.P. Moreland, *Scaling the Secular City,* (Grand Rapids: Baker: 1987).
- Josh McDowell and Bob Hostetler, *Beyond Belief to Convictions*, (Wheaton, Illinois, Tyndale House, 2002).
- Barna Research group, *Third Millennium Teens*, (Ventura, Calif., The Barna Reseearch Group, Ltd, 1999).
- McDowell and Hostetler, *Beyond Belief to Convictions*, (Wheaton, Illinois, Tyndale House, 2002).
- Lorraine Ali and Lisa Miller, "The Secret Lives of Wives," *Newsweek,* July 12, 2004.
- David Limbaugh, *Persecution,* (Washington, D.C., Regnery Publishing, 2003).
- David Aikman, *Jesus in Beijing*, (Washington, DC., Regnery Publishing Company, 2003).
- Timothy Smith, *The Seven Cries of Today's Teens* (Brentwood, TN, Intergrity Publishers, 2003).
- Charles Swindoll, *David,* (Nashville, Tennessee, W Publishing Group, 1997).

- John C. Maxwell, *Think on These Things*, (Kansas City, Missouri: Beacon Hill, 1979).
- See Readings in *Harper's Magazine*, "All the Necessary Tools," (New York, New York: December, 2003).
- Dr. Kevin Leman, "Dare to Be Different," *www.family.org/pplace.*
- Plato, "Republic 12" (403c) (Jowett Translation), *Exploring Plato's Dialogues: The Life of Plato, plato.evansville.edu/life.htm.*
- David Orland, "When Music Is Our Enemy," *www.boundless.org.*
- *http://lyrics.com/*
- Our View, "Broken Marriages, Not Gay Nuptials, Pose Risk to Kids," *USA Today* (February 23, 2004).
- Bob Waliszewsk, "Grandparenting Through the Murky World of Pop Music," (October/November 2000), *LifeWise Webzine, www. Family.org.*
- James Dobson, "Eleven Arguments Against Same-Sex Marriage," (May 23, 2004), CitizenLink,*www.family.org.*
- Steve Jones, "Combs and Bad Boy have it good," *USA Today*, (March 9, 2004).
- Barbara Whitehead and David Popenoe, *The State of Our Unions 2002*, The National Marriage Project, Rutgers University, June 2002.
- Steve Jordahl, "Is the End of the Family Near?" (March 17, 2004), *www.family.org.* Ravi Zacharias *I, Isaac, Take Thee Rebekah,* (Nashville: W Publishing, February 2004).
- Robert H. Bork, *Slouching Towards Gomorrah*, (New York, ReganBooks, 1996).